Nicholas Nickleby

adapted from the novel by Charles Dickens

by Jonathan Holloway

Samuel French — London
www.samuelfrench-london.co.uk

NICHOLAS NICKLEBY

First presented by Red Shift Theatre Company on Thursday 4th October 2001 at The Maltings Arts Centre, St Albans, and on tour throughout the UK with the following cast:

Smike **Miss La Creevy** **Lord Verisopht** **Charles Cheeryble** **Gride**	Darren Hawkes
Nicholas Nickleby **Pluck** **Brooker**	Stephen Lucas
Kate Nickleby **Fanny Squeers**	Kate Rawson
Mrs Nickleby **Mrs Squeers** **Madeleine Bray**	Susan Swanton
Squeers **Sir Mulberry Hawk** **Ned Cherryble** **Snawley**	James Traherne
Ralph Nickleby **Vincent Crummles**	Mario Vernazza
Newman Noggs **Pyke** **Frank Cheeryble** **Bray**	Tim Weekes

Directed by Jonathan Holloway
Designed by Neil Irish
Original Music by John Nicholls

COPYRIGHT INFORMATION

CHARACTERS

Nicholas Nickleby, optimistic, well educated young man of about 19. Standard English with a hint of Devon

Pluck, dissolute venomous affected friend of Sir Mulberry Hawk

Brooker, Ralph's old accomplice, a former gentleman, now a coarsened and dishevelled ex-convict

Ralph Nickleby, Nicholas's embittered uncle

Vincent Crummles, hugely theatrical actor-manager

Kate Nickleby, Nicholas's sister, well-educated, intelligent and sensitive

Miss Fanny Squeers, daughter of Dotheboys headmaster, coarse, ignorant young woman with no experience of the world and a very high opinion of herself

Mrs Squeers, coarse, ignorant and violent, villainous headmaster's wife

Mrs Nickleby, Nicholas's widowed mother, naïve, unworldly and always chattering

Madeline Bray, intelligent, sensitive and Nicholas's future wife

Newman Noggs, Ralph's clerk

Pyke, affected and dissolute friend of Mulberry Hawk

Frank Cheeryble, handsome and pleasant nephew of the Cheeryble brothers

Bray, selfish, sickly father of Madeline

Smike, simple, oppressed life-long victim

Miss La Creevy, cheerful, lonely portrait painter and landlady

Lord Verisopht, decent but weak noble in Hawk's power

Charles Cheeryble, oddball twin, Nicholas's benefactor and saviour

Gride, elderly usurer with designs on Madeline

Squeers, ignorant, violent Yorkshire headmaster

Sir Mulberry Hawk, monstrous manipulative usurer

Ned Cheeryble, the other oddball twin, Nicholas's benefactor and saviour

Snawley, slimy assistant in Ralph's corrupt schemes

Extras: **Boys**

SYNOPSIS OF SCENES

The action of the play takes place in various locations
in Yorkshire, Portsmouth and London

Time — Victorian (but can be updated at the director's
discretion, please see note below)

NOTE ON THE TEXT

This stage version of *Nicholas Nickleby* was first produced by Red Shift
Theatre Company in 2001. It toured throughout the UK. Directed by
writer Jonathan Holloway, designed by Neil Irish and with original
music by Jon Nicholls, the production was set in England in the 1950s
in order to link Dickens's campaigning themes with the 20th Century's
post-war decline of deferential attitudes towards the establishment. An
effort was made to give some of the language contemporary resonance.
This ought not to discourage the producer wishing to site the play in the
19th century world of the original novel.

Jonathan Holloway

NOTE ON CASTING

The original cast list appearing at the front of this edition indicates it
is possible to perform the play with a minimum cast of M5 F2 with
doubling.

Other plays by Jonathan Holloway
published by Samuel French Ltd:

The Dark
Darkness Falls
Les Misérables
The Monkey's Paw
The Railway Siding

ACT I

SCENE 1

Noggs is on stage

Noggs What to tell? And how much about myself? That I was once a gentleman, I suppose. That my life was a happy one and I had respect, professional standing and money in the bank. And then I was ruined by circumstance ... No that's wrong. (*Pause*) I'm being kind. (*His temper flares*) He doesn't deserve that. When it comes to the matter of judgement, you see — death, like old age, really shouldn't be taken as a mitigating circumstance. It was him ruined me, and then made me his servant and familiar. (*Pause*) Oh how it drags on day in, day out. Crafty avarice grows rich, while honest manly hearts are made poor and sad. (*Pause*) Forgive me. It's just ... so hard to know where to start. Well ... Childhood never leaves one, does it? Then let's go to school. To the aptly named Dotheboys (*pronounced "Dutherbies"*) Hall. In Yorkshire.

SCENE 2

Dotheboys Hall

Mrs Squeers, Boys and Nicholas are on stage. The Boys are seated at furniture standing in as desks, all very afraid and looking down

Mrs Squeers Good-morning, Mr Nickleby.
Nicholas Good-morning, Mrs Squeers.
Mrs Squeers You're early.
Nicholas I thought I'd give myself a chance to look around. Umm ... What's that you're giving the boys?

Squeers enters. He carries a cane

Squeers Morning, Nickleby. You're early.
Nicholas Yes.
Squeers Well, good. Well done, I suppose.
Mrs Squeers He was asking about the green liquor.

Squeers It settles the boys. Now, that can't be bad, can it?

Nicholas I didn't say it was. Bad, I mean.

Mrs Squeers We want you to be a success here, Nickleby. But if that's going to happen, you'll need to get used to us. This is a progressive school, Nickleby. In which we combine tradition and innovation.

Squeers And science.

Mrs Squeers Exactly. They have the green liquor partly because if they didn't they'd always be ill, and getting worked up, and so on.

Nicholas I ... see.

Squeers (*taking Nicholas to one side*) I'll be honest with you, if you're man enough for it.

Nicholas Yes, I think I am.

Squeers Good. Most are bastards or handicapped or both. Payment — when payment's made — covers for many things. We found it most effective when advertising "no vacations" — if you take my meaning? And the green liquor helps all around. No wantings, yearnings. A peaceful little community. No memories of home. She's a marvel, Nickleby. Does things for the boys I don't believe half their own mothers would.

Nicholas I don't doubt it, sir.

Squeers Help me into my gown, would you? That's right. Gown's an important thing, isn't it?

Nicholas Yes. Where did you study, sir?

Squeers (*after a pause, eyeing Nicholas coldly*) Because it lets everyone know where they stand.

Nicholas Yes. Of course. (*Pause*) The tall fellow?

Squeers Who?

Nicholas The boy at the front of the class.

Squeers Smike? He's an idiot. I choose the word deliberately not pejoratively. An idiot who understands less than the average mongrel. Now, let's to it. This is our centre of excellence, Nickleby. (*Turning to his wife*) Is the medicine over with?

Mrs Squeers Just finished. And don't they look the better for it.

Squeers For what we have received, may the Lord make us truly thankful.

Boys Amen.

Nicholas It's a very small class, isn't it?

Mrs Squeers These are the boys who need special help.

Nicholas They're very quiet.

Squeers Indeed.

Nicholas It doesn't sound in the least like any schoolroom I'm used to.

Squeers Good. I say, "good, and the point has been proved".

Nicholas (*confidentially*) It's very cold in here.

Squeers (*confidentially*) You can fetch down your knitteds later.

Nicholas (*confidentially*) What about the boys?

Squeers (*confidentially*) We don't allow 'em. Spoils the uniform look of the boys. Besides, you mustn't overheat boys. All kinds of trouble. Chilliness slows 'em down. (*Out loud*) We go according to the practical mode of teaching, Nickleby. The vocational educational system, as I call it. C—L—E—A—N. Clean.

Boy Verb active — to make bright — to scour.

Squeers W—I—N. Win. D—E—R. Winder — a casement. When the boy has learned this, he puts the two together, goes outside and does it. And in that way both boys and institution benefit. Weeds and garden. Cows and milkin'. And so on. Both progressive and profound. I should publish, Nickleby. I really should. What do you think, Nickleby?

Nicholas It sounds ... a very useful approach.

Squeers (*eyeing Nicholas with suspicion*) I believe you.

Squeers removes two letters from his inside pocket, both of which have been opened.

I was about to tell you to earn your keep, Nickleby. With an hour or so of hearing 'em read. But you've won a reprieve. Letters from home, you see?

There are murmurs from the boys

Boys, I've been to London, and have returned to my family and you, as healthy as ever.

The boys give a feeble cheer — all eyeing Squeers' cane.

I have visited the education department, and the school has received an excellent report, you'll be glad to hear. I have also met the parents of some boys, and they're so pleased to hear how their sons are getting on, they tell me there's no prospect of their boys being taken away.

Pause — silence

Mrs Squeers That's a very pleasant thing to reflect upon, don't you think?

Squeers But there were disappointments. Bolder. There's a letter here from your father. He's two pounds short. Where is Bolder?

Boy's voice Please, sir. Here he is.

Squeers Come here, Bolder.

Bolder approaches

Squeers uses the cane to raise the boy's hand to the horizontal — ready for punishment

Now you just listen to me ... (*Looking at the Bolder's hands*) What do you call this?

Bolder I can't help it, sir.

Squeers Warts.

Bolder They will come. It's the dirty work, I think, sir. At least I don't know what it is, sir. But it's not my fault.

Squeers Bolder. You're an incorrigible scoundrel. And as the last thrashing did you no good, we will see how well another will do toward beating your scoundrel ... ry, out of you.

Bolder Please don't hurt me, sir.

Squeers lashes the boy across his palm

Squeers And the other one. Ah, warts there too. Well, let's see if we can't knock them off. Keep your hand still.

Squeers pauses for a moment, tormenting the boy with anticipation, then lashes his other palm

Nicholas Mr Squeers!

Mrs Squeers Quiet, Nickleby. Don't confuse the boys.

Squeers Now sit down. And shut up. Next one. Cobbey. Stand! Cobbey's maiden aunt is dead.

Mrs Squeers Maiden aunt, indeed.

Squeers There's eighteen pence enclosed. Which the school will take, Cobbey. To pay for the pane of glass Webster broke. That's shared responsibility, boys.

Boys Shared responsibility, sir.

Squeers An important lesson. (*Confidentially to Nicholas*) Not his maiden aunt at all. His maiden mother, in fact. Goes for lots of 'em. Embarrassment on two legs, humiliation at the table.

Nicholas You mean the poor boy's mother ...

Mrs Squeers Shh! Don't make a thing of it. Don't give 'em an excuse.

Squeers We want no dramas, Nickleby. No dramas, here.

SCENE 3

The schoolroom, evening

Nicholas and Smike are on stage

Nicholas Smike? Is it you? Don't shrink away. I can't stand it. You mustn't be afraid of me. (*Pause*) Are you cold?

Smike No.

Nicholas You're shivering.

Smike I'm not cold. I'm used to it.

Nicholas Please, you need not be afraid.

Smike Don't be kind. That makes it worse. You'll break my heart.

Nicholas Shhh. How old are you? Are you a man yet?

Smike By years? I don't know. So many years. A long time since I was a child, though. I was younger than any here. Where are they now?

Nicholas Who are you talking about?

Smike My friends. They are all long gone.

Nicholas Don't lose hope, Smike.

Smike Hope. There's none for me. Did they tell you about the boy who died?

Nicholas What? Recently?

Smike The headmaster said he died just to spite the school.

Nicholas The headmaster ... Well ...

Smike I was with that boy at night, and when it was all silent he cried no more for friends to come and sit with him. He saw faces from home crowded around his bedside. He said they smiled and talked. He died lifting his head so his mother could kiss him.

Nicholas Yes.

Smike What faces will smile upon me when I die? Who will talk with me in the darkness? If they came from my home, I wouldn't know who they were.

Nicholas Do you remember anything about life before you came to Yorkshire?

Smike No faces. Sometimes, I feel, but don't see, the man who left me here. One thing, though. Long, lonely nights in a small high room. And in the ceiling, a small window, through which the moon sometimes stared. And a big iron hook ... in the ceiling ... next to the latch of that window.

Nicholas (*after a pause*) Is that really all you can remember?

Smike (*offering a pitiful shrug of his shoulders*) Pain and fear. That's all. Pain and fear is all there is for me.

SCENE 4

The staff room

A few threadbare upright chairs. Nicholas is resting, reading a book at the end of the day

Mr and Mrs Squeers enter

Squeers Nickleby.

Nicholas Oh, good-evening.

Mrs Squeers What did you think of your first day?

Nicholas I think the job is going to ... test me.

Squeers Not necessarily a bad thing.

Nicholas No.

Mrs Squeers How are your quarters?

Nicholas I'm not particular.

Mrs Squeers (*under her breath*) That's lucky.

Nicholas I was wondering. Does the boy Smike ever get letters?

Squeers Smike? Not a word. And there never will be. Been left here all these years, and not a penny paid after the first six. And not a clue who he belongs to either. We were caught out there. I won't take an anonymous boy again.

Mrs Squeers Nor have you.

Squeers Nor have I, that's right, my dear.

Mrs Squeers Will you eat with us this evening?

Nicholas I'm not sure. I feel I've got a lot to do.

Squeers All work and no play makes Jack a dull boy, Nickleby. Mrs Squeers sets an impressive table. All thanks to the boys, eh?

Mrs Squeers Our daughter Fanny will be joining us after supper. She doesn't eat with us. Claims it's not seemly.

Nicholas Why?

Mrs Squeers She's a young lady. And she doesn't like others seeing her nibbling, and biting and chewing. She thinks it's not nice.

Nicholas I think I'll look after myself this evening, if that's all right.

Mrs Squeers Shame. We thought a few words might be useful. (*Pause*) I can tell you straight, Mr Nickleby, I wasn't happy with your appointment.

Nicholas I'm not sure I know quite why I'm here. Except that, following my father's death, we have become dependent on my uncle Ralph. And it is he, and your husband, who settled on this position.

Mrs Squeers So it's all down to Ralph Nickleby, is it? I thought so. Why does he want you out of the way? And for how long?

Nicholas Pardon? Out of the way?

Squeers Mr Ralph Nickleby is a man of business, with a great many delicate enterprises about him. He's put plenty of boys our way. In order to help settle the affairs of those who can't look after 'em. Your presence isn't a burden, Nicholas. Not unless you make yourself one. No, you're a kind of sign. You signify a compact.

Nicholas Perhaps I ought to leave.

Squeers After I paid to get you all the way up here, and advanced you a salary for the benefit of your family? I don't think so.

Nicholas If you assume I am so naked in the world that I cannot offer you recompense, then you are both insulting and incorrect.

Squeers I would remind you that your mother and your sister are dependent on Mr Ralph Nickleby. He told me how he was angry at having you all dumped on him. How for tuppence, he'd unload you all with a "good riddance".

Nicholas He said that?

Squeers And I think he'd reckon you've set out to cross him if you turned up back in London. He doesn't like you, you know. Not one bit. Told me all about how you cheeked him on the subject of your waster of a father. How you made faces at him and clenched your fists. Just like you're doing now.

Mrs Squeers Remember your place, sir. That you are poor, and obliged to regard us as your superiors.

Nicholas Madam, I object to your ——

Fanny Squeers opens the door and enters in all her glory

Squeers Fanny!

Silence

Mrs Squeers Fanny. You look a picture. Doesn't she, my dear?

Squeers Of course she does.

Fanny And you'll be the new man. Mr Nickleby.

Nicholas That's right.

Lights fade on the action, leaving an area DC which becomes Fanny's "stage"

Squeers and Mrs Squeers exit

Nicholas remains in the darkness Fanny comes to the front of the stage and talks to the audience. She is very excited

Fanny You must keep my secret. Do you promise not to tell? It's just all so exciting, and delicate. Well, the truth is, if I'm not actually engaged, it's as near as a human can be without a ring to show for it. And to a gentleman's son who has come as a teacher to Dotheboys Hall under most mysterious and remarkable circumstances. Indeed, I have divined the cause of events. The matter has come about through a business connection between my father and his uncle. And somehow the fame of my beauty coursed along this connection, and indeed, he came to Dotheboys precisely because of the fame of my many charms and accomplishments. Determined to seek me out and win me. Can you credit such a thing? Don't ask me what he said, my dear. If you had only seen his looks and smiles. I never was so overcome in all my life. I do so palpitate. Agh!

Fanny flees the stage

Nicholas walks on to the darkened space. Alone and ruminative. He stands staring into the darkness, then remembers something. He searches his pockets, his case and finally the pocket of his overcoat, where he discovers an envelope

Nicholas Someone to do with my uncle, no doubt. (*Reading — having to hold it up to the faint interior lighting*) "My dear young man. I know the world. Your father did not, or he wouldn't have lent me money when there was no hope of return. You do not either, or you wouldn't have let your uncle pack you off to the North ..."

Nicholas continues to read

Noggs walks forwards out of the darkness, places his hand on Nicholas's shoulder and speaks out loud the contents of the letter

Noggs "If ever you want a shelter in London — and don't be angry at the suggestion, I once thought I never should either — go to the Crown in Silver Street, nearby your uncle's house in Golden Square. Ask after me there. They know where I live. Of course, you can come to my apartment at night. Although I should say there was a time when no one was embarrassed to visit Newman Noggs. But never mind that. That's all over."

Nicholas (*reading*) "Yours, in faith, Newman Noggs."

Noggs "PS If you should happen to visit Barnard Castle in Yorkshire, then ask for a pint of ale at the King's Head. Say my name, and they won't make you pay. You may say my name there, because I was a gentleman then. I was indeed."

Nicholas' head droops forward as he finally cries — afflicted by the awfulness of Dotheboys, and touched by Noggs' letter

SCENE 5

Miss La Creevy's lodging house

Kate Nickleby sits for a portrait executed by Miss La Creevy, her spinster landlady

Miss La Creevy And when … (*Concentrating on her work*) When do you expect to see your uncle again?

Kate Soon, I hope. This state of uncertainty is unbearable.

Miss La Creevy I suppose he has money, doesn't he, Kate?

Kate Yes. I believe he is very rich, Miss La Creevy.

Miss La Creevy You may depend on it. Otherwise he wouldn't be so rude. When a man is that unpleasant, he's generally pretty well off.

Kate I have heard he was disappointed in early life. Or maybe had his temper soured by some calamity. I am trying not to think ill of him until I know he deserves it.

Miss La Creevy Why doesn't he make your mother and yourself an allowance? A hundred a year wouldn't matter to him at all.

Kate I don't know what it would be to him. But I would rather die than take it.

Miss La Creevy What on earth do you mean?

Kate He has made statements, Miss La Creevy. About my father. My father who was cautious, until mother persuaded him to invest — because it was the fashion. My father who was made bankrupt while the company directors escaped on their "limited liability". My father, who managed his modest resources to educate his children, nurture his family and provide an income for many others in our little corner of Devonshire. My father who died because he could no longer protect us, and it broke his heart. I only ask that my uncle Ralph will make a little gesture on my behalf, and enable me, on his recommendation, to earn — literally — my bread, and remain with my poor silly mother.

Ralph enters stealthily

Ralph Ladies.

Miss La Creevy Oh! (*Springing up*) Mr Nickleby. You quite surprised us.

Ralph Your servant, ladies. You were talking so loudly that I was unable to make you hear. Is Mrs Nickleby about?

Miss La Creevy I'll fetch her for you, sir.

Miss La Creevy exits

Ralph Your mother claims my brother died of a sadness.

Kate And I believe that too.

Ralph There's no such thing as a broken heart. I can understand a man dying of a broken neck, or suffering a broken bone. But a broken heart. Nonsense. It's the cant of the day. If a man can't pay his debts, he dies of a broken heart, and suddenly his widow's a martyr.

Kate Some people, I believe, have no hearts to break.

Ralph Don't bark at me, young lady. (*Pause*) I ... see my brother in you. Perhaps. And there should be some softness ... Don't you think?

Kate And what of Nicholas? Didn't you see the resemblance in him too?

Ralph Young women. You're a damnable problem, aren't you? Do you know what a lure is?

Kate Yes. I think so.

Ralph It's shorthand for a "young woman".

Miss La Creevy enters

Miss La Creevy She's pleased to say "Mrs Nickleby will be here directly".

Ralph Is she, really? Pleased, is she? (*Pause*) Is that my niece's portrait, ma'am?

Miss La Creevy Yes it is, Mr Nickleby. It will be a very nice portrait too, though I say it, who am the painter.

Ralph Don't bother to show it to me, ma'am. I have no eye for likenesses. Is it nearly finished?

Miss La Creevy Why, yes. Two more sittings. Are you interest —

Ralph Then you'd better be quick. She'll have no time to idle after tomorrow. Work. We must all work. Have you let their lodgings yet, ma'am?

Miss La Creevy I haven't put the notice up yet, sir.

Ralph Put it up at once, ma'am. They won't want the lodgings after this week. I have made alternative arrangements. (*Pause*) You're very silent, niece.

Mrs Nickleby enters

Mrs Nickleby My dearest Ralph.

Ralph But there's one who'll make up for you. (*To Kate's mother*) I have found a situation for your daughter, ma'am.

Mrs Nickleby Well! Now, I will say that is only just what I have expected of you. "Depend upon it," I said to Kate only yesterday morning at breakfast, "after your uncle has provided in the most ready manner for Nicholas, he will not leave us until he has done at least the same for you." These were my very words as near as I can remember. Kate, my dear, why don't you thank your ——

Ralph Let me proceed ma'am, pray.

Mrs Nickleby Kate, my love, let your uncle proceed.

Ralph I have procured a place for you, ma'am. With a West End couturier.

Mrs Nickleby A dressmaker. Oh, dear.

Ralph Yes. What's the matter? Don't look like that. I don't know what a dressmaker might be in Devonshire, or wherever, but in London it is a couturier — a person of great wealth and fortune.

Mrs Nickleby Really?

Ralph The lady's name is Mantalini. The establishment is called Chez Mantalini. She lives near Cavendish Square.

Mrs Nickleby In Cavendish Square?

Ralph Yes. (*Pause*) Very nearby.

Mrs Nickleby Marvellous. At last the clouds have parted. I can see the way ahead, illuminated by the sunbeam your uncle has provided.

Ralph I'm glad you feel that way.

Mrs Nickleby Kate will surely make a success with Madam Mantalini, wouldn't you agree, brother-in-law?

Ralph I've no reason to think otherwise.

Mrs Nickleby And there will be a time when the proprietress of such an establishment, worn out by the cares of presentation and art, must pass the reins to a trusted successor. And there is no reason why that shouldn't be you, Kate. In fact, you may be a partner in no time at all. Say thank you to your uncle, Kate.

Kate I am very much obliged to you, Uncle.

Ralph I'm glad to hear it. I hope you'll do your duty. And now, I'm going. Business — a word with which my dear brother was barely acquainted.

Mrs Nickleby I fear that's true. In fact, if it hadn't been for me, I don't know what would have become of him.

Ralph (*to Kate in confidence*) No point remonstrating with her. No point, Kate. Good-day, ladies.

Ralph exits

Miss La Creevy (*after a pause*) I am afraid it is an unhealthy occupation. I recollect getting three young milliners to sit for me when I first began to paint, and I remember they were all very pale and sickly.

Mrs Nickleby Oh, that's not a general rule by any means. I remember employing one a good few years ago. She was particularly recommended, and wore a scarlet cloak. At the time when such things were fashionable. She had a very red face.

Miss La Creevy Perhaps she drank. But you're not to worry. If there is no other heart that takes an interest, Mrs Nickleby, there will be this one lonely woman to pray for your daughter both day and night.

Mrs Nickleby Really? (*Pause*) How kind.

SCENE 6

Early evening

Nicholas is walking in the open air, obviously distracted with worries. He passes Fanny Squeers perched upon a wall. Obviously waiting, but feigning disinterest

Nicholas Good-evening.

Fanny (*to herself*) He's going. I shall choke. (*Out loud*) Come back, Mr Nickleby, do. Come back, Mr Nickleby.

Nicholas Is there something wrong?

Fanny (*suddenly inspired*) Oh, I feel a little faint. Please ... Your arm. (*He offers it*) Thank you.

Nicholas What is it?

Fanny Nothing. The fence. I felt a little odd. The height I think. (*Laying her head on his shoulder*) So foolish. To climb so high. But I've always been an adventurous sort. (*Pause*) Reckless, even. Are you a reckless fellow also? Are we at one in that?

Nicholas (*gently but firmly disengaging himself*) I'm sorry. I'm afraid I am not in the mood for mirth just now. I wouldn't make good company.

Fanny What do you mean?

Nicholas What do you mean, what do I mean?

Fanny I mean you made it clear from your manner last night that you longed for a quiet moment together, and I have been sitting there these past forty-five minutes in order to accommodate you. And now you answer my efforts with an "I wouldn't make good company", if you please.

Nicholas I am very sorry if I have misled you in any way. If I did so, then I am very angry with myself for confusing you.

Fanny That's not all you've got to say, surely?

Nicholas (*embarrassed pause*) You don't think ... Do you imagine I have developed an attraction toward you?

Fanny It's all right. Don't look so worried. You're a little forward perhaps. But there! It's out in the open.

Nicholas Stop! Listen to me. You've made a mistake. This is only the second time I've seen you.

Fanny What?

Nicholas But if I'd seen you sixty times, the situation would still be the same. I don't want to hurt you. But you must understand, I hate this place. I regard it, and its associations, with loathing and disgust. I don't know you, Miss Squeers. You may be the best of young ladies. But the fact is I detest your father and the horrors he has perpetrated here. There is nothing about this place which inclines me to romance, I'm afraid.

Fanny (*very quietly*) Are you refusing me?

Nicholas I'm afraid so.

Fanny (*flintily*) Refused by a teacher picked up in an advert, and at a salary of five pounds a year.

Nicholas Miss Squeers. Please. This is a delusion.

Fanny is enraged, and displays a degree of mental instability

Fanny Refused by a boy given "found" lodging and food, like the children he teaches. (*Pause*) Me, attracted to you? No. I hate you for your narrow mind and your violent temper. How dare you make overtures to me. I reject you, utterly. Such an odd creature. (*She reaches for a stone from the wall in a threatening manner — obviously deranged*) I don't feel safe in your company. Damn you! (*She is about to brain him, but stops herself, is overcome by an eerie calm and carefully replaces the stone with an oddly studied precision*) No. I won't let you do that to me. You'll pay a high price for this. Or ... someone will pay it on your behalf.

SCENE 7

Miss La Creevy's lodging house

Noggs has come in order to accompany Mrs Nickleby and Kate to the new cheaper home provided by Ralph

Noggs The conveyance is outside.

Mrs Nickleby "Conveyance". Ah, you see your uncle has sent a cab to transport us to our new home.

Noggs A van for the boxes. We're to walk.

Mrs Nickleby No. Surely not.

Kate How far is it?

Noggs (*quietly, to Kate*) Couple of miles. (*To Kate's mother*) It's a fine day. It'll give a chance to sight-see. There's a fellow with the van. (*Rubbing his fingers to indicate money is involved*) He's waiting.

Mrs Nickleby Well, I suppose we'd better get on.

Noggs D'you need a hand down the steps?

Mrs Nickleby Not necessary. (*Leaving*) Besides there's not enough room for both on the stairs at one time.

Kate What is our new accommodation to be?

Noggs Style or quality?

Kate Both, I suppose.

Noggs It's from Mr Ralph Nickleby.

Kate Meaning?

Noggs Don't expect too much. It's the cheapest he could find. (*Pause*) And I'm sorry about it. (*Pause*) Now Noggs must get on. (*He makes to leave*)

Kate Excuse my curiosity, but didn't I see you at the coach station on the morning my brother went away to Yorkshire?

Noggs (*still facing away from her*) No.

Kate Pardon me. But I should have recognized you anywhere.

Noggs Well, you're wrong. This is the first time I've been out for weeks. I've had a poisoned toe.

Kate Where are we going, Mr Noggs?

Noggs (*still with his back to her*) Into the city. We'll turn down to the riverside, and after about a half an hour wash up at a dingy old house in Thames Street. I think you will consider is has been uninhabited for some years. There was a dead dog in the hallway. But I moved it yesterday afternoon.

Kate Thank you.

Noggs You're welcome.

Kate You are being kind to us. Why?

Noggs Don't suspect me, Miss Nickleby. I don't want anything. Sometimes, when a thing has gone on for too long. A way of dealing with people, so to speak. There comes a time when someone's got to draw a line. And say "no, I'm not going to allow it".

Kate Are you talking about my uncle?

Noggs That man's waiting with his van. We'd better go down.

Kate and Newman Noggs walk to the front of the stage and survey the auditorium as if we are the front of the dilapidated house Ralph has assigned to his relatives

Kate This house depresses and chills one, and seems as if some blight had fallen upon it. If I were superstitious, I would be inclined to believe that some dreadful crime had been perpetrated within those old walls, and that the place had never prospered since. How frowning and dark it looks.

Mrs Nickleby advances DS *to join them*

Noggs is staring at the floor

Mr Noggs. We needn't detain you any longer.

Noggs (*still looking at the ground*) Are you sure there's nothing I can do?

Kate Nothing, thank you.

Mrs Nickleby Perhaps, my dear, (*she fumbles for a coin*) Mr Noggs would like to drink to our healths.

Kate I think, Mother, you would hurt his feelings if you offered it.

Scene 8

Dotheboys Hall

Nicholas discovers Smike poring over a book which evidently makes no sense to him. Smike mouths the words as best he can, but tears of frustration run down his cheeks. Smike glances up and recognizes Nicholas

Smike I can't do it. No, I can't. No matter how hard I try.

Nicholas Then don't try. It's all right. Don't. Please. I can't bear to see you so unhappy.

Smike (*closing the book*) They are more hard with me than ever.

Nicholas Shhh. Not so loud. They punish you to spite me. Fanny ... Well, she is behind most of it. She has convinced her mother to hate me as much as she does, and goads her father to beat you harder each day. Squeers resents our friendship, and the way I teach.

Smike Are you going?

Nicholas I can't stay, can I? I'm making it worse for all you boys. And there's nothing to be done to change Squeers.

Smike You don't mean it. Tell me, please. Will you go?

Nicholas Quiet. Shhh. Calm down.

Smike (*after a pause*) Is the world as bad and dismal as this?

Nicholas No, Smike. The worst I've seen couldn't hold a candle to this place.

Smike Will I ever meet you out there in the world?

Nicholas Yes, of course. Nothing lasts for ever.

Smike So, I shall be sure to find you?

Nicholas Yes. And I shall be able to help you, and not bring fresh sorrows with me as I have done here.

The Lights snap to a cold dawn

Smike scuttles away

Boys, including Tomkins, enter rubbing the sleep from their eyes

Nicholas also rubs his eyes

Squeers sweeps on stage with his cane

Squeers You lazy hounds.

Nicholas We shall be down directly, sir.

Squeers Yes, you'd better be. Or I'll be dealing out thrashings every-which-way. Smike! Where is he? Nickleby!

Nicholas Yes, sir?

Squeers Smike. Where is he? I need him for scrubbing out.

Nicholas He's not here, sir.

Squeers Of course he's not here. Where have you hidden him? Where is he?

Nicholas At the bottom of the nearest pond for all I know.

Squeers Damn you, what d'you mean by that?

Tomkins Please, sir, I think Smike's run away, sir.

Squeers Who said that?

Tomkins Tomkins, please, sir.

Squeers You think he has run away, do you, sir?

Tomkins Yes, please sir.

Squeers And what reason do you have to suppose that any boy would want to run away from this establishment?

Squeers knocks Tomkins to the floor with a stunning blow which makes the onlookers gasp. Nicholas makes a slight movement towards Squeers but checks himself. Squeers has noticed and fixes Nicholas with a threatening stare

Now if any other boy thinks Smike has run away, I'll be glad to have a talk with him. Well, Nickleby? Does that include you?

Nicholas I do think it very likely he has run away.

Squeers Oh. You do, do you? Maybe you know for certain he has?

Nicholas No, I don't. If I did, then it would have been my duty to warn you.

Squeers You're proud, aren't you, Nickleby? And maybe that rubs off on the boys. Now, I want you to take the boys off to the schoolroom, and I don't want you or them stirring out of there until I give the say-so. I don't care if it's two o'clock in the morning, you'll stick at your lessons until I say otherwise.

Nicholas Yes.

Squeers "Yes." Exactly. I wouldn't want to fall out with you in a way that might spoil your beauty — handsome as you are.

Nicholas and his complement of boys make their way upstage — backs to the audience. Squeers walks to the front of the stage, then turns his back firmly to the auditorium

Smike shuffles slowly on

Squeers stretches out a hand and grips him by the collar. Smike allows himself to be gripped

Mrs Squeers enters and stands, cutting off Smike's escape

The three figures downstage are silhouetted as Nicholas and his class turn towards downstage and stare aghast at the image of the captive Smike

Squeers Is every boy here? Each boy keep his place. Nickleby, stand still sir! Smike. Do you have anything to say for yourself? (*Pause*) No, of course not. (*Pause*) Stand back a little, my dear. I need room to get a good swing at him.

Smike Please. Don't kill me, sir.

Squeers (*laughing*) Of course I won't kill you, Smike.

Mrs Squeers Not quite, anyway.

Smike I was driven to running off.

Squeers Oh, it wasn't your fault, it was mine I suppose, eh?

Mrs Squeers A nasty, ungrateful, idiotic, obstinate, sneaky little animal.

Squeers We had a boy once, used to hit himself with a spoon at the table. Blind, deaf and stupid. He enjoyed it. His idea of a good time. Now, I'm going to give you the best old time ever, Smike.

Nicholas Stop.

Squeers
Mrs Squeers } (*together*) What?

Nicholas You've done enough. The boy will die of heart failure if you're not careful.

Squeers freezes for a moment then in slow motion lets his shoulders slump as if surrendering. Then, in a flash he draws back the cane and swipes Smike so hard the boy staggers and cries out in pain, like a wounded dog

No!

Nicholas launches himself at Squeers. He shouts his lines as he labours with the cane against both Mr and Mrs Squeers. The company of boys leap forward and hold Mr and Mrs Squeers fast

You will not. Shall not. Bully and torture these children any more. I will not stand by and see it done.

Mrs Squeers God in heaven, you've killed him.

Nicholas (*voice trembling at the magnitude of what he has done*) Boys! Clear out all of you. Get your things and go. Run, and don't stop, in case they try to blame any of you.

The Boys scatter

Nicholas backs away, leaving Mrs Squeers crying, hunched over her husband's still form. He is about to exit when she suddenly looks up

Mrs Squeers Don't think you'll get away with it. You'll be hanged for this.

The stage is empty for a few moments

Then we watch Nicholas, as if in a dream, wander into view and slump by the roadside. Smike approaches nervously

Nicholas Smike. Get away from me. For your own sake. I don't want you punished for my actions all over again. (*Pause*) What do you want, Smike?

Smike To go with you. Anywhere. Everywhere. To the world's end. To the churchyard grave. You are my home. My kind friend. Take me with you.

Nicholas Poor you. And poor me. If each can't do better than the other.

CURTAIN

ACT II

SCENE 1

London, outside Newman Noggs's apartment

There is an explosion of activity and noise representing the two men's arrival in London

Nicholas and Smike look very wet and bedraggled. Nicholas confronts Newman Noggs at his apartment door. Smike does his best to hide behind Nicholas. There is a long, awkward pause

Noggs Mr Nickleby. Better late than never. You'd better come in. You're wet through. And I'm sorry to say I don't even have a set of spare clothes for you to change into.

Nicholas I have some dry clothes. As much as I need, anyway. (*Pause*) You don't look very happy to see us. I'm sorry. Look, this is very embarrassing. I took you at your word ... What you said in the note. Could you at least tolerate us for one night?

Noggs On the contrary, sir. I don't intend you should feel unwelcome. I wouldn't have offered sanctuary if I didn't mean it. I'm just not used to things working out. It's been some while since they have. And who's that behind you?

Nicholas Step forward, Smike.

Noggs Why doesn't he speak? What's the matter with him?

Nicholas He's a poor chap from that infernal Squeers establishment. His name's Smike, and he's a frightened fellow who's used to being beaten whether he says yes or no.

Noggs No doubt you'll come out of yourself when you're ready, Mr Smike. For now, I'll make you a promise, you'll not be beaten while I've got anything to do with it. Come in and sit down, Mr Smike.

Newman Nogg's room is conjured through the arrival of a couple of upright chairs and a low level amber uplight representing a fireside

They are all soon settled by the fire

Nicholas My family? Are they still living in the city?

Noggs They are.

Nicholas And my sister? Is she still employed by that lady with the exotic name?

Noggs Madam Mantalini. So you came here first. Before seeing them.

Nicholas It is for the best. Circumstances will follow me here which might place my family outside the law, were they to shelter me. Tell me, and don't spare the truth ... what have you heard from Yorkshire?

Noggs Not good.

Nicholas I understand. I am prepared to hear the very worst.

Noggs Tomorrow morning. Hear it tomorrow.

Nicholas What good would that do?

Noggs You would sleep soundly tonight.

Nicholas I can't hope to sleep tonight unless you tell me everything. I can hardly bear to think of it. Although I was driven to the act, yet the law and men's judgement will be against me. (*Hardly able to say the word*) A murderer.

Noggs (*aghast*) Who did it?

Nicholas What?

Noggs The murder. And who was killed?

Nicholas Me. I am the perpetrator.

Noggs Heavens! And who did you kill?

Nicholas Squeers, of course. God help me.

Noggs Then it seems he has. By helping Squeers back from the dead.

Nicholas What?

Noggs Your uncle received this letter the day before yesterday. Listen. "Sir. My father requests me to write to you. The doctors consider it doubtful he will ever recover the use of his legs, which makes it impossible for him to hold a pen ..."

Nicholas Alive? He's alive, then?

Noggs Shhh.

The figure of Fanny Squeers hovers in the half light on the edge of the room

Fanny My father is one mask of bruises. After the nephew you recommended as a teacher had beaten his face unrecognizable, he jumped on him with both feet. Then he assaulted my mother with dreadful violence, throwing her to the floor with terrible force. Having sated his thirst for blood, and assuming my father killed by his hand, the monstrous young man turned coward, and ran from the scene accompanied by a desperate character whose violent fits and threatening demeanour has, for years, been the prime focus of my father's remedial efforts — out of compassion for the tortured soul lurking behind the barbarian features of the boy known only as

Smike. As if your nephew's sin were not enough, the Judas stole my mother's wedding ring, presumably to finance his flight from justice. Speaking of which, my father informs me that, out of compassion for you, he will not press charges, as he does not blame you for the stain of villainy which Mr Nicholas Nickleby has brought upon your house. Return of the ring, and some compensation for lost revenue from the escaped boys, would be appreciated at your convenience. I remain your, Fanny Squeers.

Fanny retreats into the dark, outside the circle of firelight

Nicholas Mr Noggs. I must go out at once.

Noggs Out? Where? Supper will be ready soon.

Nicholas The fact Squeers lives reprieves me. But I must go to my uncle's house, at Golden Square. I have to tell him the truth, and exchange a few other words which he deserves to hear.

Noggs You must not go.

Nicholas I must.

Noggs There's no point. He's away from town. Won't be back for three days.

Nicholas Are you sure of this?

Noggs Quite. He only had time to scan the letter, before he was called away. When he gets back we'll engineer to have you appear before your family at the exact moment he conjures to confront them with the story of your violence. That will be your chance to speak the truth strong and true before everyone.

Nicholas I don't like to proceed by stratagems. It makes me uneasy.

Noggs Stratagems are exactly what you're mixed up in here. And you'd better get a sense of 'em, or you're not going to last the game out. And that reminds me, you need a new name. If you're to go about without Mr Ralph Nickleby's many ears reporting your presence, then you can't use the name you were born with. So what's it to be?

Smike Johnson!

Noggs and Nicholas jump at this unexpected contribution

Noggs Johnson?

Nicholas Why Johnson, Smike?

Smike It was Mr Johnson and Johnson on the bottle of the green stuff they gave us to make us not want to eat. And to stop us dreaming.

Noggs (*after a pause*) Poor fellow.

Nicholas Indeed. But Johnson sounds good to me. And you, Noggs? Strikes me you've made a dangerous choice here. Setting yourself against your employer.

Noggs That's assuming he ever guesses. And I intend he shouldn't, until he hears the click of the trap behind him.

Nicholas Noggs. Don't cross him.

Noggs Noggs will cross that man every way he can, and leave no trace of it, Nicholas Nickleby. That's the game I've settled on.

SCENE 2

Kate is dressed as though for a very special social occasion. She is alone, and nervously paces the room

The dull sound of indistinct male voices can be heard coming from an adjacent room

Ralph enters, flushed and in a hurry

Ralph I couldn't see you before, my dear. I had to meet them as they arrived. Now, ready? (*Pause*) Shall we go through?

Kate Uncle. Are there any other ladies here tonight?

Ralph No. I don't know any.

Kate Then, do I have to go in right now?

Ralph That's up to you. They're all here, and dinner will be announced directly. And you are here, at my request and expense, in order to ornament that dinner. That's understood, isn't it?

Ralph draws Kate's arm into his, and they walk downstage

   A throng of dinner guests, including Verisopht, Hawk, Pyke and Pluck, assembles upstage of the couple, who turn to signal their entrance

Ralph (*loudly enough to draw everyone's attention*) Lord Frederick Verisopht. My niece, Miss Nickleby.

Verisopht Eh! (*Adjusting his monocle, then very impressed*) What the deyvle!

Ralph My niece, my lord.

Verisopht (*liking the look of what he sees*) Then my ears didn't deceive me, and she's not from out the g-g-gallery. How d'you do. I'm very happy to meet you.

Kate sits on an upright chair C

   (*To the other men, with no effort to hide his lasciviousness*) Deyvlish p-p-pritty.

Hawk Nickleby, where are your manners? Introduce me.

Ralph Sir Mulberry Hawk.

Verisopht Watch out, Miss Nickleby. The sharpest card in the p-p-pack.

Pyke Don't leave me out, Nickleby.

Ralph Mr Pyke.

Pluck Nor me, Nickleby.

Ralph Mr Pluck.

Verisopht An unexpected p-p-pleasure, you certainly are, Miss Nickleby.

Pluck No doubt calculated to throw you off your guard, my lord.

Hawk Seize the moment, Nickleby. Mark his lordship down for another twenty-five, and up the rate by a couple of per cent. (*He laughs, but we can see he means it*)

Verisopht Take no notice of 'em, Miss Nickleby. If I was half the dupe they said, I'd barely be able to p-p-put one foot in front of the other. Now, will you accompany me into d-d-dinner.

Hawk (*imitating Verisopht*) No, d-d-damn it, Verisopht. Miss Nickleby and I settled I'd take her in, just with a look between us.

Pyke Ha! Very good.

Pluck (*to Verisopht*) She's left you out, my lord.

Pyke Indeed.

Kate But I ——

Hawk What, my dear? (*Pause*) Ah, there's an acre of meaning in a woman's cry, isn't there? Careful you attend to your dinner, my lord. And don't mind Miss Nickleby and I. We shall be most absorbed, you see?

Verisopht This fellow Hawk is going to monopolize your niece, Nickleby.

Ralph He already has the lion's share of everything you lay claim to, my lord.

Verisopht God! So he has. Deyvle knows who's master in my own house.

Ralph I think I do.

Verisopht There's nothing to do but cut him off. Not a shilling more, Hawk.

Hawk When it gets down to the last shilling, then I'll cut you off fast enough. Until then, we're inseparable friends.

Pyke (*in confidence*) You know, Pluck, what's remarkable about Hawk isn't his talent for ruining young aristocrats.

Pluck (*in confidence*) Isn't it?

Pyke (*in confidence*) No. It's the fact he allows them to enjoy it so much.

Pluck (*in confidence*) A talent, indeed.

The assembly freezes, and is backlit while music indicates the passage of time

Lights up on a company congratulating themselves for having dispatched mountains of food and wine

Hawk Here is Miss Nickleby wondering why on earth somebody doesn't make love to her.

Kate No indeed.

Hawk I'll bet any man here fifty pounds that Miss Nickleby can't look me straight in the face, and tell me that's not what she was thinking.

Pyke Done. But we'll put a time limit on it. Ten minutes. For me to win, she has to look you in the face and tell you to push off within the next ten minutes.

Ralph Fifty pounds. That's a lot. (*In confidence*) Kate. Go carefully. Sir Mulberry Hawk is money in the bank to me.

Kate (*in confidence*) Please don't make me the subject of any bets, uncle. I am not used ——

Ralph (*in confidence*) Don't be silly. It'll be done with in a moment. (*Out loud*) Come, Kate. If the gentlemen insist on it.

Hawk I do insist. But not that Miss Nickleby should make the denial, of course. But even if she did, though I lose, it would be worth it to look into those bright eyes which have spent the entire evening studying the floor.

Verisopht Yes, that is too bad of you, Miss Nickleby.

Pyke Quite cruel.

Pluck Horridly cruel.

Hawk No, I don't care if I lose. One look into those eyes would be worth twice fifty. How goes my enemy, time?

Pyke Four minutes gone.

Hawk Ah, Miss Nickleby. Damned if you do, damned if you don't.

A long pause

Pyke Eight minutes gone.

Hawk You see, Nickleby. Your niece and I have an understanding. Get your money ready, Pyke.

Kate finally musters the courage to look Hawk in the face

Kate You were wrong, Sir Mulberry.

She gets up and stalks from the room

Hawk is momentarily angry, but hides it beneath a veneer of bonhomie

Hawk Capital! That's a girl with spirit and we'll drink her health.

SCENE 3

Ralph's library

Kate is seated on a sofa in Ralph's library, pleased to be away from the men. She studies the contents of a book while waiting for her uncle. Hawk enters unnoticed

Hawk What delightful studiousness.

Kate How did you get up here?

Hawk Were you really reading the book, or was that for my benefit? To show off your eyelashes. Luscious innocence, eh? You know the tricks, don't you?

Kate How long have you been in here?

Hawk Five minutes. You are perfect, my dear.

Kate Please don't say anything more. Just go.

Hawk Don't be so hard on such a devoted slave. Don't treat him so unkindly.

Kate I want you to understand that your behaviour offends and disgusts me. If you have an ounce of pride in yourself, then please leave immediately.

Hawk What game are we playing? Why this indignation? Be more natural. My dear Miss Nickleby. More natural. (*He now has his arms about her*)

Kate (*struggling*) Let me go. Right now. Let me go this instant.

Hawk Sit down. (*Forcing her on to a sofa*) Sit. I want to talk to you. Just to talk.

Hawk's hand has gone to the hem of her skirt, which he is gathering upwards

Kate Oh, God. No. Please, no.

Ralph enters

Ralph What's this?

Kate forces Hawk to let go of her. She stands and he sprawls awkwardly half on the sofa, half on the floor

Kate "This?" I should have found protection here. I should not have been exposed to the insult, which I see by your face, makes you unable to look upon me.

Ralph (*to Hawk while pointing at the door*) That's the way out!

Hawk Have you forgotten who I am, and what we are to each other? (*Pause*) Ahh, I see. You wanted the young lord, didn't you? Damn it. I got in the way and spoiled your plot, didn't I? Well, who brought him to you? Who helped you wind him in a net of debt?

Ralph Be careful of that net. If I chose to, I could foreclose and ruin you. And although I'd feel it, I'd survive all right.

Hawk Are you trying to tell me you didn't bring your niece here to draw that drunken boy closer in? If he'd found his way up here instead of me, you would have been slower up those stairs, and a little more blind and deaf.

Ralph Maybe I did bring her here as a matter of business.

Hawk That's the word! You're recovering your wits, then?

Ralph I thought she might make some impression on that silly boy you're working so hard to ruin. And by so doing, bind myself further into your process of desiccation. But I did this knowing the only offences he might perpetrate would be awkwardness, puppyish humourless humour and emptiness. If I had thought my niece would be subject to the brutality you intended here, I would never have brought her.

Hawk Especially when there's no money in it, eh?

Ralph (*quietly surrendering*) Exactly so.

The two villains stand, staring at each other, each knowing exactly what the other is about

Hawk leaves

Kate dissolves into tears so violent she seems unable to catch her breath. Ralph is suddenly frightened by the severity of her reaction

Quiet, my dear! Hush. Don't let it upset you so much. There's no harm done. Try not to think about it.

Kate For pity's sake, let me go home. Let me leave this house, and go home.

Ralph Yes. Of course you shall go, instantly. But first you must recover your composure. We can't let those villains know what's happened here. Not even a rumour of it. Let me dry your eyes. There!

Kate What have I done to you to deserve this? What have I done? What is it about me that makes you want to drag me down, and see me stained and spoiled? That is your intention. Isn't it?

Ralph Of course not. Come on. There. Sort you out. That's it. Now you look yourself again. Yes.

Kate Please. Send me home.

Ralph Yes. Of course. Just a moment for your tears to dry.

Ralph finds himself staring into Kate's face, transfixed

Ralph You look so like him.
Kate Who?

Ralph backs away from her

Ralph My brother. I called him into the garden, and he ran to me. I swung the chair and caught him in the face. Why?
Kate Why did you trick him? Is that what you mean?
Ralph Why does a life ...? (*Pause*) Go now. By the back way. (*Suddenly nasty*) GO!

SCENE 4

The Nickleby residence

Music and lights convince us of a passage of time. Mrs Nickleby joins Ralph and Kate, and the three characters arrange themselves for a confrontation at the Nickleby residence

Ralph (*brandishing Fanny Squeers's letter above his head*) This is good, don't you think? Yes, very good. I recommend the boy — against my considered judgement — to a respectable man in whose employment Nicholas might have remained for years to come. And what is the result? Actions in return for which we might have expected to see him in dock at the Old Bailey.
Kate I don't believe it. This is some trumped-up conspiracy against my brother.
Ralph My dear girl, these aren't inventions. The man Squeers is assaulted, your brother is fled, along with this gibbering lunatic boy, Smike.
Kate No. I won't believe it. And the stolen ring. Impossible. My brother isn't a thief. It's a trick to squeeze us. Mother! How can you tolerate these slights?
Mrs Nickleby Oh, dear. That things should have ended up like this.
Ralph If he comes near me, it will be my duty to give him up to the police. And yet. (*Fixing Kate with a stare*) I suppose I might not do that. In order to spare the feelings of his sister.
Kate (*conspiratorially*) I take that as an inducement not to reveal the events of last night.
Ralph (*conspiratorially*) Take it for whatever you damn well like.

Nicholas enters without knocking or announcing himself. Everyone is surprised

Nicholas Whatever he has told you ... I swear it is a lie.

Kate runs to restrain him, while Ralph backs away in fear of Nicholas

Kate Nick. Don't make things worse.

Nicholas When I consider what you have done to me, I want to squeeze the life out of you.

Mrs Nickleby Oh, Nicholas. What will become of you?

Nicholas Of me? What has he said to poison you against me? He who sent me to a den where arbitrary cruelty ruins children, blighting their lives. I have seen it, and that man knows exactly what I'm talking about.

Kate Calm down, Nick. Don't give him a chance to condemn you. Tell us what really happened.

Nicholas I interfered to save a miserable and degraded creature from the vilest cruelty. In doing so I was forced to inflict punishment upon the headmaster which I am sure he will not readily forget. If the same scene were to be renewed here and now, I would do it again, but I would hit him harder and heavier, and take that poker from that fire and brand him with marks he would carry to his grave.

Ralph So, Kate. This is an apology, is it?

Mrs Nickleby My son! I just don't know what to think. I really don't.

Kate Mother, please. Just for once try not to be blown every-which-way, but stick fast to what you know — that Nick is honest. Nick, they accuse you of theft. They say a ring is missing.

Nicholas Squeers's wife dropped a worthless trinket amongst my clothes early on the morning I left. I found it when I opened my bundle on the road. I posted it back.

Kate Good. I knew it. And this boy they say is dangerous, and mad?

Nicholas The boy is actually a man. A kind and affectionate creature made silly and helpless by brutality and hard use. He's with me at ... at my lodgings.

Ralph So, everything is proved. Will you restore that boy to the establishment entrusted with his care?

Nicholas No, I will not. I wish I knew who had given him birth, then abandoned him to incarceration and abuse. If only I could make that man look into his scarred, bewildered face. And if he didn't weep for his sin right there, then I'd make him.

Ralph Fine. That's good. You missed your vocation, I think. It's surely politicians who, like you, employ flights of oration to excuse their own sinning. Now listen to me, everyone here. (*To Mrs Nickleby*) And especially you, madam. I have made promises for the upkeep of your daughter and yourself. I fully intend to honour them. But I say that this boy will not have use of one penny of my money. I will not take his hand, even if it is to drag him from the gallows. I will not meet him, visit where he visits or help those who help him. I will not permit him to be a burden on you or my niece. I am concerned for your daughter's future, but I cannot care about him. There is beauty and grace in her which I care for. (*Pause*) Don't look like that, young man. I have had enough of young women's plots and games in my life, so don't worry on that account. The Mantalinis were in debt to me, but the arrival of unexpected debtors from the past has obliged me to foreclose on them to save a penny in the pound. That means your job, Kate, has disappeared. But I shall find you another. Because we must all work for our bread. Now, I believe that makes things clear. (*Addressing Mrs Nickleby*) And so, without prejudice, I place our friendship, and consequently your future, in your own hands.

Mrs Nickleby I can't do it. I can't renounce my own son. Even if he has done all that you say he has. We shall pack our things and go to the council, or to the streets, Kate.

Nicholas No. He's been clever, and he's won this round. You don't have to leave here. I will ensure his conditions are met, because I'm going away, Mother.

Kate No. I couldn't bear for us to be apart again.

Nicholas We shall not forget each other when we're apart. And better days will bring us back together. I am no help just now, but as God is my witness, I shall be back. (*Indicating Ralph to step aside with him*) And now I have something to say which is only for you to hear. Whatever you do now, it shall be recorded in my account book. I leave them entrusted to your care, and if you break faith with that, I shall come back and break you.

Ralph Fine.

Nicholas Fine.

Ralph, Kate and Mrs Nickleby leave Nicholas alone on stage

Smike appears and approaches him with trepidation

Nicholas Ah, Smike. Cheer me up, will you? Tell me what new sights you have come across, and which new friends you have made today.

Smike No. We must talk of something else.

Nicholas Certainly, Smike.

Smike I can see you're unhappy, and I know that bringing me to London has got you into trouble. I ought to have seen that would happen. You haven't any money. Not even enough to feed yourself, let alone me. You're thinner. Pale. Your eyes have sunk into your head. I can't bear

it. I tried to go today, but your face, in my mind ... it brought me back.
I couldn't leave without saying goodbye.

Nicholas I refuse that word, Smike. I shall never say it to you. You are my
best friend. My very best. I wouldn't lose you now, for all the world. You
show me what goodness and forbearance mean — and so you are my
example. Give me your hand. (*He takes Smike's hand and places it flat on
his own heart*) Two men, and yet one heartbeat. We're leaving London,
Smike. I don't care about being poor. We'll be poor together, eh?

SCENE 5

Outside an Inn

*One scene melts into the next. Nicholas and Smike, equipped for
travelling, stand at an inn door talking to the Landlord*

Nicholas Still twelve miles to go, you say?

Landlord Twelve long miles. That's right.

Nicholas Is there much traffic?

Landlord Not at this time. And none that will take you.

Nicholas I do need to get on, though.

Landlord Of course, it's your choice. Personally, I'd wait until tomorrow.

Nicholas Would you?

Landlord Especially if I was on to a good thing. (*He indicates the
inside of his pub*)

Nicholas I suppose so. All right, we'll stay. What can you give us for
supper? And remember we're ... on a budget.

*Nicholas and Smike divest themselves of their gear and sit before a
glowing fire. Gradually Smike falls asleep*

*Vincent Crummles enters the room carrying a jug of beer and some
glasses*

Crummles (*speaking in a booming "theatrical" fashion*) Mind if I join
you, young man? (*Indicating the beer*) I'll bring my welcome with me.

Nicholas That's very kind.

Crummles My name is Crummles. Vincent Crummles.

*He looks at Nicholas as if expecting to hear "not the Vincent Crummles",
but Nicholas just stares back in a friendly manner*

And yours is ...?

Nicholas Nickle ... as. Nicholas. Johnson. Nicholas Johnson.
Crummles And that fellow there?

Smike is asleep in his chair

Nicholas That's Smike.
Crummles "Smike". Unusual. Punchy. I like it. "Smike".
Nicholas He's tired, and his health isn't good. And that fine meal the
    landlord found us has just bowled him out.
Crummles (*settling himself in a chair and pouring beer*) Are you on
    the way to Portsmouth?
Nicholas Yes.
Crummles Do you know the town, at all?
Nicholas No.
Crummles Never there?
Nicholas Never.
Crummles You know, I hope you won't mind me saying, but your
    friend has an excellent face.
Nicholas Poor fellow. I wish it were a little more plump and less haggard.
Crummles Plump? No. That would spoil it.
Nicholas Do you think so?
Crummles Just as he is, right now, he'd make such an actor for any
    starveling business you like. Better than anyone else I've seen. He'd
    hardly need any make-up. Just a little five and nine, and a spot of
    carmine, to bring him out.
Nicholas Ah-ha! You're looking at him with a professional eye, then?
Crummles Yes indeed, and I never saw a young fellow so positively
    cut out for character work since I joined the profession at the age of
    eighteen months. (*Pause*) What's the matter? I can see you're uneasy.
    What are you hoping for in Portsmouth?
Nicholas Finding something to do which will keep my friend and I.
Crummles Ah. "Your friend". Now I catch on.
Nicholas What?

*Crummles taps the side of his nose as if to say, "don't worry, it's just
between us"*

    No. You've got it wrong.
Crummles You mustn't worry. I'm in the theatre. That kind of thing ...
    we don't worry about it.
Nicholas I am Smike's guardian. That's all.
Crummles Fine. No really. That's fine. So what do you expect Portsmouth
    has to offer?

Nicholas I take it there are many vessels leaving port. I shall try for a working berth on board a ship. That will at least provide meat and drink.

Crummles If your stomach can take it.

Nicholas One could do worse. And I'm prepared to rough it.

Crummles You'd better be, if you do go on board ship. But you won't.

Nicholas Why not?

Crummles Because there's not a skipper who would think you worth your salt when he can get a practised hand. Seamen are born to it. It's not something you just pick up overnight. Isn't there anything else that appeals to you?

Nicholas I can't think of anything to suit a man with a little education, few friends and even less sense.

Crummles I can. The stage!

Nicholas (*incredulous*) The stage?

Crummles The theatrical profession. I am in the theatrical profession, my wife is in the theatrical profession, my children are in the theatrical profession. I had a dog that lived and died in it, and my pony makes regular appearances — most recently in *Tamburlaine the Great*. I'll put you on stage. And your friend too. We need a novelty. Just say the word.

Nicholas I haven't acted a part since I was at school.

Crummles There's genteel comedy in your walk and your manner. Juvenile tragedy in your eyes. Touch-and-go farce in your laugh. You'll do as well as if you'd thought of nothing else but the lamps from your birth. We shall open our new show in a few days' time. New and splendid scenery. A real pump and two wash tubs. I bought 'em cheap and we'll get them in somehow. Think of it on the posters. Real pump! Splendid tubs!

Nicholas What shall I earn?

Crummles Pardon?

Nicholas Could we live on what I earn?

Crummles Live on it! Like a prince. Together, your friend and yourself, you'll make a pound a week.

Nicholas Really? No. That much?

Crummles Indeed. And if we have a good run of houses, I guarantee you'll double it. Your hand?

Nicholas offers his hand

Nicholas Indeed, sir. Done!

Smike (*stirring*) What is it? What's the matter?

Nicholas You have a profession, Smike. You're to be an actor.

Smike Oh, indeed? Really. (*Pause*) What's an actor?

Crummles Mr Johnson. Do you speakee zee French?

SCENE 6

The stage is transformed into a footlit down-at-heel weekly rep. Nicholas and Crummles are alone on stage

Crummles Forgive me, Mr Johnson, if I'm a little slow to get going. Theatrical hours don't like an early rising, you know. Well, maybe when we're in the first flush, like yourself. But us old-stagers ... and I'm a family man too.

Nicholas Don't worry. I'm a little the worse, myself. It was an excellent party last night.

Crummles "Party?" That wasn't a party. Just a little gathering. A welcome to Portsmouth for your friend and yourself. Mind you, theatricals! Never know when to stop. Did you have a chance to look at the French play?

Nicholas Yes. It looks very good, I think.

Crummles And free. How's Monsieur what's-his-name going to know, eh? Now then, is there anything in it for me? Anything in the way of gruff and grumble?

Nicholas You turn your wife and child out of doors, and in a fit of rage stab your eldest son in the library.

Crummles Excellent. Sounds like just the part for you, Nicholas. Father and son. We'll make a good pair.

Nicholas After which you are troubled with remorse until the last act, and then you make up your mind to destroy yourself. But just as you are raising the gun to your head, a clock strikes   ten.

Crummles I see. Very good.

Nicholas You pause. You recollect you have heard a clock strike ten in your infancy. The gun falls from your hand ...

Crummles From my hand ...

Nicholas You are overcome. You burst into tears.

Crummles (*wailing*) OH GOD IN HEAVEN!

Nicholas And become a virtuous and exemplary character forever afterwards.

Crummles Capital! But what about you? Do you come back on?

Nicholas No. I'm dead.

Crummles As a ghost then, dear boy. I think we must write in some incident allowing you to appear as an angel. Someone passed over to the other side. We have a white suit. Well, not quite what you'd call white any more. But no one will notice from the third row back. It will make you very romantic. Now then, is there a dance?

Nicholas No.

Crummles I must have a dance of some kind, you know. Works both ways, the young folks giggle and the mature ladies sigh.

Nicholas I'm sorry, I just can't see where it would fit.

Crummles You astonish me. It's easy. The young man — you, in fact — lies there, dead on the library floor. His distressed mother sinks into a chair and buries her face in a pocket handkerchief. Please don't weep, Mama, says the little child whose unexpected arrival has brought such joy to the mature couple — my daughter, of course. "You'll make me weep too, Mama." "Oh, Pierre" — it's French, so I assume I'm "Pierre" — "Oh, Pierre", says the bereaved good lady. I may be able to arouse myself after some small diversion that will help me to suffer with fortitude. Do you remember the dance, dearest Pierre, which in happier days you practised with this sweet little girl of ours? And there you have it. Cue the band on "sweet little angel of ours", and I'll be on my toes directly.

Nicholas Are we seriously doing this tonight?

Crummles Of course.

Nicholas There's not a lot of time, is there?

Crummles Ah, you forget. The rest of the performance will be made up entirely from turns — that means the best scenes from other plays. The performers know them already. It's their repertoire. This will be the only demanding part of the programme. We shall rehearse the vignettes shortly — including Smike's contribution — and devote the afternoon to our innovations.

SCENE 7

Crummles is rehearsing his actors, who are dressed as follows — Smike as Verisopht, Crummles as Ralph Nickleby, Mrs Nickleby as Mrs Nickleby and Hawk as Hawk

Crummles Now then, I don't like to rehearse too much. Diminishing returns, you see. Just so long as everyone knows what happens and in what order. As I explained, the evening will consist of one full story and selections from melodramas. Our second favourite is a scene from *The Hawk*. And this is the one you've been practising, Smike. (*Pause*) Smike?

Smike Yes?

Crummles Are you ready, Smike?

Smike No.

Crummles Good. Nicholas, we'll rehearse you in a half hour or so. Moving on. Moving on. So now we shift the location. (*Shading his eyes and staring at the lighting box*) Can we have the next location? (*He gives up on the lighting box, and looks for stage management in the wings*) No. (*Shrugging*) Apparently not. The old reprobate (*indicating Hawk*) and the malleable young lord — that's you, Smike — find the old money lender — that's me, Smike — at home.

Hawk Ah. Alone, eh? Well I know you're not pleased to see me, after our altercation the other night. It was his lordship wanted a word. I'll wait in the next room. Don't take too long, my lord. The cards are already dealt on The Mall.

Hawk makes a swaggering exit

Crummles (*as Ralph*) Yes, my lord. How can I help you?

There is a long pause. No one speaks. Smike has obviously lost the plot

Nicholas Smike.
Smike Yes?
Nicholas It's your turn, now.
Smike Oh. I beg your pardons.
Crummles Just get on, there's a good fellow. Don't worry, we're right with you.
Smike (*as Verisopht*) Nickleby, what a pritty creature your niece is.
Crummles (*still out of Ralph's character*) Don't forget to stutter, my boy. I always insist upon a stutter when playing aristocrats.
Smike (*as Verisopht*) P-p-pritty.
Crummles (*firmly back in character as Ralph*) Is she, my lord? I can't say I noticed.
Smike (*as Verisopht*) I want to know where this beauty lives, that I may have another p-p-peep at her, Nickleby.
Crummles (*as Ralph*) Really?
Smike (*as Verisopht*) I don't want Hawk to hear.
Crummles (*as Ralph*) So, he's your rival, then?
Smike (*as Verisopht*) Where does she live, Nickleby, that's all? Just tell me where she lives.
Crummles (*as Ralph*) No good can come of your knowing. She has been virtuously and well brought up. Does that make an impression on you, my lord?
Smike (*as Verisopht*) Yes, I suppose it does, sort-of-thing. But that's not what I'm about here. (*Conspiratorially*) I'm under instructions, do you see? But I want to fool old Hawkey. You tell me where she is, and I'll keep it to myself. Guaranteed.
Crummles (*as Ralph*) If I do tell you, you must make me two solemn promises.
Smike (*as Verisopht*) G-g-go on, then.
Crummles (*as Ralph*) That you will keep this information to yourself.
Smike (*as Verisopht*) Exactly. And what's the second?
Crummles (*as Ralph*) That the next time you need to extend your borrowing, you'll come to me, not Hawk.

Smike (*as Verisopht*) Done, Nickleby. As they say, a change is as good as a rest. Now ...?

Crummles (*coming out of character again*) And this is where I give you the address of the little house I have made over to the niece and her mother. And I also inform you of where the young lady has been engaged as companion to a horribly affected little bourgeois. (*Addressing the company*) And I tell you all, without a shadow of a doubt, at that moment there will be ejaculations in the auditorium.

Mrs Nickleby enters the room, followed by Hawk

Ha! Unexpected, eh?

Mrs Nickleby Terribly sorry, brother-in-law. I know it is a liberty to disturb you.

Hawk "Brother-in-law?"

Crummles (*back in character as Ralph*) Perhaps you could wait a moment. In the next office?

Hawk No need, Nickleby. We wouldn't want to inconvenience this delightful creature. And would I be correct in assuming you are ... Mrs Nickleby?

Mrs Nickleby (*instantly seduced*) Why that's correct, sir.

Hawk Impossible.

Mrs Nickleby No, I assure ——

Hawk But you're far too young to be ... No, it's a silly idea.

Mrs Nickleby What is?

Hawk Such a young chit as yourself couldn't possibly be mother to Mr Ralph Nickleby's delightful niece — Kate?

Smike (*as Verisopht*) Upon my soul, it's the most excellent thing. How de d-d-do?

Hawk (*conspiratorially*) Has he told you?

Smike (*as Verisopht*) Erm ... no.

Hawk (*conspiratorially*) Then stand back and leave the old trout to me. (*Out loud*) Introduce us, Nickleby.

Crummles (*as Ralph*) Lord Verisopht. And Sir Mulberry Hawk.

Mrs Nickleby Oh, I say! If I'd known, I'd have ...

Hawk And how is Miss Nickleby?

Mrs Nickleby She is quite well, I'm obliged to you, my lord. But she wasn't well for some days after she dined here. I think she caught a cold in the Hackney coach which brought her home. Hackney cabs are such nasty things, it's almost better to walk, don't you think? I believe a Hackney cabman can be prosecuted for life if he has a broken window. I once had a swelled face for six weeks from riding in a Hackney cab.

Crummles (*as Ralph, after a pause*) Is that letter for me?

Mrs Nickleby And I walked all the way up here on purpose to give it to you.

Hawk What a confounded inconvenience. Now, how far would that have been?

Mrs Nickleby Let me see. It's about a mile from our door to the Old Bailey.

Hawk As much as that?

Mrs Nickleby It is. Down Newgate Street, Cheapside, up Lombard Street, Down Gracechurch Street, as far as Spigwiffin's Wharf. Oh, it's definitely a mile.

Hawk And surely you don't mean to walk all the way back to Spigwiffin's Wharf?

Crummles (*as Ralph*) Why not? In fact, you'd better get a move on before the streets get too thick with going home.

Hawk Exactly the reason we should accompany you, young lady.

Mrs Nickleby "Young lady".

Hawk Verisopht?

Smike (*as Verisopht*) Indeed. We'll be your pavement bargers, Mrs Nickleby.

Hawk Goodbye, Nickleby. Bagatelle, I think!

Hawk, Verisopht and Mrs Nickleby leave Ralph by himself

Crummles (*as Ralph, turning out to the auditorium*) God! How ugly. Selling a girl — throwing her in the way of temptation, insult and coarse speech. But Verisopht is already worth two thousand to me. And don't matchmaking mothers do the same thing every day? If I hadn't put Verisopht on the right track, this foolish woman would have done it without my help. Well. If her daughter is as true as her demeanour suggests, she'll come to no harm. A little teasing. A little humbling. A few tears. No one will die from it. No, she must take her chances. (*He turns away, then stops in his tracks, milking the moment. He turns back to the audience, ashen-faced*) She must take her chances, mustn't she?

SCENE 8

Ralph's office

Ralph stands motionless in the fading light of his office

Kate knocks sharply

Ralph Who's that?

Noggs Me. (*Pause*) Your niece.
Ralph What about her?
Noggs She's here.
Ralph Here! What does she want?
Noggs I don't know. Shall I ask?
Ralph No. Show her in.

Kate enters, proud and angry, but near to tears. Her appearance gives an ambiguous impression of what she is suffering. Her demeanour indicates she has been physically abused by Hawk and Verisopht

Ralph Well, well, my dear. What now?
Kate The reason which brings me to you should make you burn to hear it. I have been wronged. And all this has been done by your friends.
Ralph I have no friends, girl. Besides, where's the harm? I'm sorry for the tears, but the whole escapade will have been an excellent lesson.
Kate If they weren't your friends, but you knew their intentions, then it shames you even more, uncle, that you brought me among them. If you did it knowing them, then it was a horribly cruel thing to do.
Ralph You have your brother's hot blood in you.
Kate I hope so. I am young, uncle. And all the difficulties and miseries of my station have made me hold back my words. But now I say I am your brother's child and I will not bear these insults any longer.
Ralph What insults?
Kate Please. Release me from the vile and degrading companionship I am exposed to now. I have no one to protect me. My mother supposes these men are rich and distinguished. And how can I undeceive her when she is so happy in her delusions?
Ralph How can I assist you, child?
Kate You have influence over these men, I know. Would not a word from you induce them to leave me alone?
Ralph (*after a pause*) No. I can't say anything. (*Pause*) Assuming I wanted to.
Kate Can't?
Ralph We are connected in business and I can't afford to offend them. We all have our trials to put up with. This will end. Sooner or later. And some girls would be proud to have such gallants at their feet.
Kate Proud?
Ralph I'm sure you're right to despise them. But in all other respects you are comfortable, and it's not much to bear. What does it matter if this young lord whispers drivelling inanities in your ear? What of it? Some other novelty will spring up, and you'll be released.
Kate And in the meantime I am degraded in my own esteem, and in every eye that looks upon me.

Ralph As I say, my dear. I can't help you.
Kate (*backing away towards the door*) Oh, Uncle.
Ralph Come again, when you like.

Ralph leaves, and Kate runs into Newman Noggs

Noggs Don't cry. Don't cry. I see how it is. It was right for you to tell
him to his face. Yes. You poor thing. Now, don't cry any more. I shall
see you soon. And when I come, I'll have Nicholas with me. I'll take
you home.

Noggs and Kate leave the stage. Ralph comes back in

Ralph (*giving a sudden scream, as if he has been wounded*) Ahhhh!
(*Pause — then quietly*) You'll pay for this. Oh, you'll pay for this,
your lordships.

SCENE 9

A backstage dressing room

*Nicholas is visited by Vincent Crummles. Both are making-up ready for
the evening performance*

Crummles What can I say? Well done, Mr Nicholas Johnson. Your
presence has been such a success that we might remain in Portsmouth
another week. Not since the days of Alleyn and Shakespeare has a
young theatrical achieved such an immediate success both within art
and finance. I bid you *adieu*, and will see you in the wings, my dear.
Nicholas You are most gracious, Mr Crummles.
Crummles Ah Nicholas, the gaudy bows before genuine talent.

Crummles exits

Smike Twenty pounds. It's a fortune. What will you do with it?
Nicholas I already sent money to Kate and my mother.
Smike Is that safe?
Nicholas I sent it via Newman Noggs. At his home address. That will
keep it out of my uncle's way.

Crummles knocks on the dressing room door and opens it

Crummles Apologies, dear boy.

Nicholas That's all right. Come in.

Crummles No. I mean for spoiling my exit. Horrible to come on again like this. Erm ... Oh, yes. A letter, just arrived. For you, Nicholas. From London. Ah, a whiff of the city.

Crummles leaves

Drury Lane — I hear you. I hear you.

Smike What is it?

Nicholas It's from Newman. Oh, God.

Smike What's the matter?

Nicholas My enemy is about his plotting. My sister is in danger. Newman says not to come just yet, but to await his signal. How can I wait, though? If she is in danger I should be at hand.

Smike Who is your enemy?

Nicholas My uncle?

Smike Will you punish him as you did the master, Squeers?

Nicholas I don't know. This man is rich, and not so easily done down.

Smike But now you're rich, too. What is his name?

Nicholas Ralph Nickleby.

Smike Ralph Nickleby. Ralph Nickleby. I'll get that off by heart — just like my speeches.

Nicholas That's it, Smike. We leave by the morning coach. That's enough of practising our parts. Now we have the means, so we must begin our work in earnest. I have put things off for too long. And now I'm about you, Uncle. And there will be nowhere for you to hide.

CURTAIN

ACT III

SCENE 1

The den of a public house

Nicholas sits down at a table with a mug of beer. He becomes aware of a group of boisterous "gentlemen" at a nearby table

Hawk Given nobody objected to toasting her with the dregs of the last bottle, I suggest we do the same with the top of a new magnum. Especially as you're paying Verisopht. To little Kate Nickleby!

Verisopht
Pyke } (*together*) Little Kate Nickleby!

Nicholas (*to himself*) What? No. I imagined it.

Hawk And again.

Hawk
Verisopht } (*together*) Little Kate Nickleby!
Pyke

Nicholas (*to himself*) God in heaven!

Hawk The jade. She's a true Nickleby — a worthy imitator of her Uncle Ralph. She hangs back to be more sought after. So does he. Nothing to be got from Ralph unless you pester him. And by that time the funds are doubly needed and thrice welcome. Oh, what a cunning family.

Verisopht
Pyke } (*together*) Infernal cunning, hurrah!

Verisopht It appears she's gone to ground. Can't work it out. Maybe her mother's wise.

Hawk Maybe the old trout's jealous. Wants us for herself.

General laughter

Still, she believes anything I tell her.

Verisopht Egad, that's true. P-p-poor old deyvle.

Nicholas (*approaching the group*) I'd like to have a word with you, sir.

Hawk With me, sir?

Nicholas That's what I said. Yes.

Hawk A mysterious stranger, eh?

Nicholas Perhaps I have not made myself clear. I want you to step apart with me for a few moments. (*Pause*) Do you refuse?

Nicholas takes a card from his coat pocket and lays it down before Hawk

There. Now, I believe you can guess what I want to talk about.

Hawk is ashen. He sits weighing Nicholas' strength and the danger he represents

You were very vocal just now. And yet you seem struck dumb. I want your name and address, and then we can arrange an early morning encounter, I think. Perhaps near Richmond.

Hawk I shall not give you my name. Or my address.

Nicholas If there is a gentleman in this party, he should feel obliged to acquaint me with this man's name. (*Pause*) I am the brother of the young lady who has been the subject of your conversation. I denounce this person as a liar and a coward. If he has a friend here, then that man should spare this moron the disgrace of attempting to hide his identity. I will find it out. And I won't leave this man alone until I do.

Hawk Let the boy prattle. I have nothing to say to a poor boy, nor am I obliged to.

Nicholas I will know who you are. And I will follow you to your home, if need be.

Nicholas pulls up a chair, sits, folds his arms, and stares at Hawk — he obviously isn't going anywhere

Verisopht I say ... (*Pause*) Old friend, couldn't you just give him what he wants?

Hawk No.

Verisopht The evening has rather gone to p-p-ot, don't you think? Besides. He won't really challenge you. And if he does, it'll be his look out. (*Pause*) Shall I tell him?

Pyke Certainly not.

Verisopht Why?

Pyke Shhh. (*Pause*) Well, old friend. Can't quite see what purpose we're serving here. Um ... Verisopht, fancy moving on? What about cards? Dammit, if I wasn't sober enough to play before, I certainly am now.

Verisopht Well, yes. I say, though. This is all rather rum, and a little d-d-disappointing, really.

Hawk Be quiet, and go. If you must.

Verisopht In a trice. 'Night.

Pyke Hmmm. 'Night.

Pyke and Verisopht exit

Hawk feigns disinterest, and continues drinking, while Nicholas sits and stares at him. Hawk then stands, puts on his hat and picks up his cane. He leaves and Nicholas follows close behind. They both stand in the street

Nicholas Will you make yourself known to me?
Hawk No, excrement. No.
Nicholas If you climb into a cab, I will stand on the running board.
Hawk You shall be whipped if you do.
Nicholas You are a craven villain.
Hawk And you are nothing.
Nicholas I am the son of a country gentleman — your equal in birth and education, and your superior in everything else. Will you answer for your despicable conduct?
Hawk (*sneering*) To a gentleman, yes. To you, no. Now, out of the way. Here comes my cab.

Nicholas steps forward and grabs Hawk's arm. Hawk tries to shrug him off and fails. The pair are now nose to nose

Nicholas You're not going anywhere until you have told me who you are.
Hawk I'm warning you. Let go of me.
Nicholas Will you tell me who you are?
Hawk No.
Nicholas No.

Hawk raises the cane in his free hand, and strikes Nicholas across the face. Nicholas reels back, recovers, then springs forward on to Hawk. Nicholas hits Hawk in the stomach, doubling him over, then sends him sprawling with a blow to his face. Nicholas, now in a blind rage, catches up Hawk's cane and strikes him across his face, opening a large gash. He then raises it again, ready to dash out the man's brains

Voice You there! Stop. Stop, I say.

Nicholas looks up, then at the stick in his hand. He drops it, shocked at what he was about to do

Nicholas What will you devils make me into? Why will you make me like yourselves?

Nicholas runs off

SCENE 2

Ralph's office

Ralph enters in thoughtful mood. Noggs enters and stands awaiting instruction

Ralph Well?
Noggs Well. What?
Ralph What do you want?
Noggs You called me?
Ralph No I didn't.
Noggs Yes.
Ralph (*after a pause*) Has the post come?
Noggs No.
Ralph Has anything else arrived?
Noggs One.
Ralph What is it?
Noggs A letter, hand delivered.

Noggs gives the letter to Ralph who breaks the seal and begins reading

Nicholas runs to the centre of the stage — between the other two characters — he obviously exists in a different space from Ralph and Noggs. Nicholas addresses the contents of the letter straight out to the audience

Nicholas The truth of what you are is known to me now. You, who would — for the sake of furthering your business interests — expose your own flesh and blood to persecution, immorality and physical abuse. I offer no reproaches because that would imply I am giving you a chance to apologize and atone for your crimes. We shun you with disgust and loathing, and I have removed my family back to Miss La Creevy's lodging house. We do not expect to see you. I hope that every hurt you have caused to every victim you have encountered will cling to your heart like an ulcer, and cause you to cry out in shame and loneliness on your deathbed. Your nephew, by the grace of God and proud, Nicholas Nickleby.

Nicholas turns and leaves

Ralph's face shows no reaction to the letter's contents. He folds the letter and puts it in his pocket

Noggs Anything important?
Ralph What? No. It's nothing.

SCENE 3

An employment agency

Nicholas goes to an employment agency. He witnesses a strange transaction between Madeline Bray, a mysterious, beautiful young woman and a benign middle-aged man, Charles Cheeryble. Madeline approaches Charles. She is obviously upset, and keeps dabbing her eyes. The man takes out a sealed envelope and passes it to her. She is very grateful, kisses his hand and leaves. Nicholas has been gawping and suddenly has to turn and study the rows of vacancy cards. The middle-aged man begins to leave but isn't watching where he's going and collides with Nicholas

Charles I beg your pardon, young man.
Nicholas I'm sorry.

Charles smiles then makes to leave. His progress is arrested by Nicholas' desire to speak to him

Charles You were about to speak, young man. What were you going to say?
Nicholas There are a great number of ... excellent opportunities here. Aren't there?
Charles In an employment bureau? I don't think so. (*Pause*) You saw something just then, didn't you?
Nicholas Yes. But I'm sorry. I shouldn't have stared.
Charles No. You shouldn't.
Nicholas I assure you, I've forgotten the whole thing.
Charles Good.
Nicholas Except that she's very pretty.
Charles Yes, she is. (*Pause*) Dammit! What's a fellow like you doing in a place like this?
Nicholas London is a wilderness if one is without a position.
Charles Yes, it is. It was a wilderness to me, once. I came to London with only the shirt on my back. And I try to remember that. What's happened? Father dead?
Nicholas How did you know?
Charles Most common thing. And I suppose you've got a mother and brothers and sisters who look to you, eh?
Nicholas One sister.
Charles Where is Wyoming?
Nicholas In America.

Charles So, you're tolerably well educated. That makes this kind of thing worse, I'd say. If you educate a man, then you make poverty more difficult to tolerate.

Nicholas I'm not sure I agree.

Charles Are we having a debate, then?

Nicholas I don't know.

Charles (*smiling*) Neither do I. My name is Charles Cheeryble. My brother Ned and I run a business in the city. I'd like you to meet him. I'm not promising anything, mind you.

Nicholas No, that's fine. Really.

Charles Come along, then.

SCENE 4

Ralph's office

Noggs stands quite still while Ralph ambles about his office, deep in thought

The front doorbell is heard offstage. Neither of the men move. It rings again, with greater urgency

Noggs The bell.

Ralph So it is.

Noggs I'll answer it, then, shall I?

Noggs moves off towards the hallway. As he goes he regards Ralph, whose manner seems distracted. Ralph looks up and catches Noggs staring at him

Ralph If I didn't know better, I'd say I ought to watch out for you, Noggs. Wouldn't you agree?

Noggs I don't know what you mean. I'll answer the door.

Noggs exits

There is a pause, then Squeers shuffles onstage. He appears changed. He walks with a stoop and supports himself with a walking stick. He wears a dirty bandage around his head, protruding from under his hat

Ralph Why, this is a surprise.

Squeers Surprise I'm still living, I'd say.

Ralph Did you need the doctor?

Squeers Yes. And it cost a bloody fortune. But I wasn't out of pocket. I defrayed the cost among the boy's expenses.

Ralph I thought all your boys ran off.

Squeers Lots did. But lots came back, once they realized they'd nowhere to run. And a couple were arrested as vagrants, and brought back by the police. And then there's new business. One advert in the quality paper, and the indiscretions of the moneyed classes come tumbling in. We're full all over again. Makes me think how sad it is for the poor ones. It's out of their mothers and into the ditch, for the crows to peck at, isn't it?

Ralph What brings you here?

Squeers There's a parent making an action against me.

Ralph Are you really surprised?

Squeers They're damned hypocrites, though. Want the boys shunted off and forgotten, then when one of 'em gets the cough and dies, suddenly they're outraged. I don't know what they've got on me. Or if they've got anything at all. But you and I have known each other a long time, and there's been plenty of business back and forwards between us. And so I knew you'd help with advice on a lawyer, and maybe, in light of your nephew's treatment of me, something in the way of paying his fees.

Noggs is seen standing in the darkness on the edge of the space. He is obviously listening to the conversation

Ralph Would you like a chance to pay my nephew back?

Squeers On my life. If I'd the chance I'd stamp his head flat, like he tried to do with me.

Ralph Who's this boy he took off with?

Squeers Not much of a boy, at all. He might have been best part of twenty. Weak in the head. Nobody at home, if you knocked, if you understand?

Ralph And I imagine you knocked pretty often.

Squeers That's right.

Ralph When you wrote to me, you said you have no clues concerning his origins. Was that the truth?

Squeers It's fourteen years since a man brought him to Dotheboys, late one winter night. He paid five pounds and five shillings for the first quarter in advance. I guess Smike was six years old at the time.

Ralph How much more do you know?

Squeers That's it. The money was paid for six years, then it stopped. This chap had given a London address, but when it came to finding him out, of course no one knew who he was. Interesting, though. There's been some asking about him in the neighbourhood lately.

Ralph What do you mean?

Squeers I reckon they all know how useful he is. And now he's grown, they want him for cut-price labour.

Ralph Are you sure? Nothing deeper?

Squeers No.

Ralph I intend to use Smike as the means by which we shall wound my nephew. Would you like the boy back?

Squeers My wife will most probably murder him, as soon as eat her dinner.

Ralph Well, that will be your business. Now, I want you to meet someone. Come with me.

Squeers But go slow. On account of what your nephew did to me.

Ralph and Squeers leave

Noggs walks into the centre of the space, obviously anxious about what he has heard

Noggs They're not going to let the poor boy alone. Not even now. But I'll stick with it, until I get my chance. I promised that boy he'd never be beaten again. And I'll make sure of it.

SCENE 5

Ned Cheeryble's office

Ned Cheeryble is at his desk when Charles and Nicholas enter

Charles Ned. I've brought someone with me.

Ned Someone with you. Ah. Hello, there. Is this the fellow about the claim? I've talked to the docker chap's family. He understands the lighterman wasn't to blame. We really ought to be paying out ourselves, you know. I'm not looking to try and blame anyone when the company's insurance can deal with it.

Charles Yes, let the insurance deal with it. No, he hasn't come about the claim.

Ned Not about the claim? Oh, I'm awfully sorry.

Charles Nicholas Nickleby, Edwin Cheeryble.

Ned Pleased to meet you. Ned.

Nicholas Nicholas. Nick, if you like.

Ned Yes, I know.

There is a pause while the pair stare at each other nonplussed

Nicholas You're twins.

Ned We certainly are. Not quite identical. We're symmetrical. His face leans that way, mine goes this. He's right-handed, I'm left. He aims with his right eye, me with my left.

Nicholas Aim? What at?

Ned Archery, Nicholas. Newington Butts every Sunday. You must join us.

Charles Ned, you remember we were talking about old Tim Linkinwater.

Ned Yes. Mind you, I haven't had the nerve to say anything to him. Besides, what's the point if we don't have anyone else?

Charles Well, I think we have now.

Ned Really. Oh, you mean Nicholas here?

Charles Sorry, Nicholas. This is the situation. We have a fellow here called Tim.

Ned He's worked for this company since before we took over.

Charles He looks after us, reminds us what's in the diary.

Ned Keeps an eye on the balances at the end of each day.

Charles Watches the work rooms and offices. (*Suddenly exaggeratedly weary*) Deals with the lightermen.

Ned (*also exaggeratedly weary*) Deals with the lightermen.

Nicholas I understand.

Ned Thing is, he's not all that spry anymore. And although he won't admit it, he can't be in all those places as quickly as he was.

Charles We're not trying to get rid of him. But we would like a reliable person to pick up some of the work. It's a funny mixture of practical jobs and brain power.

Ned Wouldn't suit everyone.

Charles Think you might be interested?

Nicholas Really? Are you offering me a job?

Charles So, are you interested?

Ned Hang on, though. I don't remember you mentioning Nicholas. How do you know each other?

Charles Erm.

Nicholas We met at the employment bureau. About two hours ago.

Ned What? I don't understand.

Charles Nicholas's father died late last year. A bankrupt landowner in Devonshire. Sorry, Nicholas. I didn't mean it to sound so brutal. He has a mother and sister to look after. His uncle — not a very pleasant sort, according to Nicholas — set him up with a post in one of the Yorkshire schools. Which turned out to be every bit as bad as you'd expect. Nicholas ended up in a fight with the headmaster, set a whole gaggle of boys free and sort of adopted a boy who can't look after himself. That's why he was in the ——

Ned Employment bureau. I'm surprised you haven't gone to drink, Nicholas. We'll have to meet your family.

Charles Check through things.

Ned Make sure you are what you say you are. But if that's all tickety, and given my brother is completely convinced, then I think we'd be pleased to have you.

Charles And there's the matter of a house. Are you fixed at present?

Nicholas Not really. We're in a small apartment in the West End.

Charles We bought some cottages a little way back from the river. One of them is still unlet. We could offer it to your family and yourself as a supplement to your income, if that were acceptable.

Nicholas I don't know what to say.

Frank Cheeryble knocks smartly on the door and walks in

Charles This is our nephew, Frank Cheeryble.

Frank Hello, there!

Charles This is Nicholas Nickleby. He'll be joining the business.

Ned Subject to contract.

Charles Yes, of course. But he will be joining.

Frank What to do?

Charles Remember we talked about Tim?

Frank Ah-ha! Excellent. Welcome aboard, Nicholas.

Nicholas Are you an archer, too?

Frank What? (*Pause*) What have they been saying? Don't believe a word, Nick. They're a pair of old Mickey-takers, these two.

SCENE 6

Ralph's house, Golden Square

Ralph is dressed to go out into the night. On his way out he runs into Noggs

Ralph Is he here?

Noggs Been here half an hour. He's waiting downstairs.

Ralph Good. Fetch us a cab.

Noggs A cab? Where shall I say you're going?

Ralph The new Nickleby residence. Reckon they thought to give me the slip. But I've got my eyes, haven't I? It's a cottage near the river. Past London Bridge.

Noggs Will you be needing me as well?

Ralph No. I used not to need to worry about you, Noggs. But now there are some things you'd best not be party to.

Ralph leaves

Brooker enters, a shadowy figure played by the same actor who plays Nicholas. He interrupts Noggs, alone

Brooker (*pointing in the direction of Ralph's exit*) Are you anything to do with him?
Noggs Who?
Brooker Ralph Nickleby.
Noggs I work for him.
Brooker What's your name?
Noggs Newman Noggs. What's yours?
Brooker I'm Brooker.
Noggs What do you want?
Brooker To put things right. As best I can. What's he to you?
Noggs I think the answer to that question will either make a friend of you, or an enemy. Am I right? (*Pause*) Well, I'll take the risk, then. He is my employer. I was a gentleman, and I borrowed. And what he lent ruined me. I was grateful for the position, but so much has happened that now I despise him. (*Pause*) So, did I calculate correctly?
Brooker (*after a pause*) You did. I was sent down for what I did as his "representative". I've been three years in Canada. Then extradited. Spent the last year in Pentonville. He expected I'd disappear. But I didn't. And so I'm a surprise to be used well. Do you understand me?
Noggs Yes. I do. I hope I do.

SCENE 7

The Nickleby residence

Frank Cheeryble is visiting the cottage. Kate is obviously interested in him. Smike stands to one side, watching Kate. Nicholas and Mrs Nickleby are also on stage

Nicholas Everyone. This is Mr Frank Cheeryble. Nephew to the brothers Cheeryble. Frank. This is my family. My mother.
Frank I'm so pleased to meet you, Mrs Nickleby.
Mrs Nickleby Oh, dear.
Nicholas Mother, what's the matter?

Mrs Nickleby You must forgive me, young man. I have recently had a
very upsetting experience with compliments. Bestowed, I'm sorry to
say, by gentlemen purporting to be kind, but whose intentions were ...
less than one might have hoped.

Frank I'm very sorry to hear that. I shall decline compliments, then.

Mrs Nickleby Oh, no. No sense in seeing the baby gone with the bath
water. Compliments will be fine. Please, just allow a bruised heart a
little time.

Nicholas Right. (*Pause*) And this is my sister, Kate.

Frank I'm very pleased to meet you, Kate. I hope you're well.

Kate Very well, thank you.

Smike looks from Kate to Frank and back to Kate

He quietly leaves the room without anyone noticing

Mrs Nickleby Why don't you sit by Kate, Mr Cheeryble.

Frank Yes, fine. Wherever. If that's convenient, Kate?

Kate Yes, of course. Here, I'll move along.

Mrs Nickleby It gives me real pleasure to welcome you in this plain
and homely manner, Mr Cheeryble. You see, we make no display here.
No fuss. I wouldn't allow it.

Nicholas Oh, and there's one other. (*Pause. He looks about for Smike*)
Now then, where's Smike gone off to? I'm sorry, Frank.

Mrs Nickleby Perhaps he's helping lay out the tea things next door.

Kate No, Nick. I saw him go upstairs.

Nicholas (*calling upstairs*) Smike! Don't disappear, there's a good fellow.

Mrs Nickleby I wouldn't worry about Smike. We've got our guest to
think about. Mind you, I hope he is helping next door. Miss La Creevy
brought some of her china, but she couldn't stay. She left a fellow to
help tidy. I let him do a little, then sent him away. Odd sort. Wore a
glazed hat, like the conductor on the omnibus, and a wart upon his
nose, exactly like a gentleman's servant.

Nicholas Have all gentlemen's servants warts on their noses, Mother?

Mrs Nickleby Nicholas, my dear, how very absurd you are. Of course
I mean that his glazed hat looks like a conductor, not the wart upon
his nose. Though even that is not so ridiculous as it may seem to
you. We had a driver once who had not only one wart, but a wen also
— a lump on his scalp — and a very large lump it was too, and he
demanded to have his wages raised in consequence, because he found
its maintenance came very expensive. Let me see, what was I — oh,
yes, I know ——

There is a loud knock at the door

Nicholas It must be some mistake. We're not expecting anyone. Excuse me.

Nicholas gets up and goes to the door

Smike enters the room. Ralph Nickleby enters immediately, followed by Nicholas, then Snawley — who stands back out of the way

Ralph (*to Nicholas*) Be quiet, you. (*To the room*) Before that boy speaks a word, hear me. Hear me. I say. And not him. (*Directed against Nicholas*)

Nicholas I will not know that man. I cannot breathe the air that he corrupts. His presence is an insult to my sister. It is a shame to see him. I will not bear it.

Frank Stand still, Nick.

Nicholas Then tell him to leave at once. I won't have him standing there looking so self-righteous when we all know the truth of his black heart.

Frank I understand, Nick. But he's obviously got something up his sleeve. Let's hear him out, before we throw him out.

Ralph (*after a pause*) Have you done with ranting, then? Good. I come here out of humanity. I have come here to restore a parent to his child. His son, sir. Whom you have waylaid, brain-addled and guarded, with the villainous intent of robbing him, one day, of the small inheritance which might come his way.

Nicholas You can't help lying, can you?

Ralph And although we've never met — I recognize you by description. Smike! I have your father here.

Snawley steps forward

Snawley It's me, son. Your father. I did my best for you, and if it wasn't enough, then I'm sorry. I'm here to claim you, and to make you a happy life, to the best I am able.

Ralph Dry your eyes, Mr Snawley. At last you have your wish.

Snawley Hard to believe he's really before me. Really flesh and blood.

Frank Precious little flesh, I'd say.

Nicholas If you are his father, then look at the wreck he is, and tell me whether or not you propose to send him back to that loathsome den which has been his only home.

Snawley I had this boy by my first wife. I sent him for an education. The best I could afford, at the time. Then my wife and I separated. Then she told me he was dead. She got ill and wrote me a letter confessing the lie. Now she's dead. And I expected to find him in Yorkshire. I won't send him back, if he doesn't want to go. But I will have him. I swear I will.

Nicholas Tell me his real name.

Ralph You say "if he's the father". I say I have a witness who will confirm Snawley's claim. Squeers is at Golden Square right now, and will provide sworn evidence this claim is true. The description of Mr Snawley and the dates given, they all tally with Squeers' books. We can produce marriage and birth certificates accordingly.

Kate Nick. Can this really be true?

Nicholas True or not, a father's rights cannot win over common, human decency.

Ralph We have a taxi waiting. I think young Snawley here should come with us, don't you?

Smike (*clinging to Nicholas*) No. No, please. I don't want to leave you. No. Please.

Snawley advances on Smike, but Frank steps in the way

Frank I wouldn't do that. In fact, I think you'd better leave.

Ralph And who are you to make pronouncements?

Frank A friend and supporter to this family, and what's good for it. It strikes me there's no hurry here. If you do have a legal right over this boy — or rather this man — then I have no doubt you will be pleased to make the point in law, before a magistrate. That would be best, I think. Certainly, I shall assign legal representation in support of Mr Smike's wishes. Mr Nickleby, if the law ends on your side, then so be it. But due process will be observed here.

Snawley I want my son.

Nicholas Your son chooses for himself. And, at least for now, he remains here.

Mrs Nickleby I am really very sorry about all this. I don't know what would be for the best, and that's the truth. Nicholas ought to be the best judge, and I hope he is.

Snawley (*to Smike*) You are an unnatural, ungrateful boy.

Snawley leaves

Ralph (*to Nicholas*) So, you have the truth about him, now. He is the weak, imbecile son of a poor, petty tradesman. No wonder you sympathize. He matches you perfectly. I always get the better of my enemies. In time. And, by this action today, you have all entered that column in the tally book.

Ralph leaves

SCENE 8

The next day

Charles Cheeryble and Nicholas are in conversation

Charles Frank has reported the whole business.

Nicholas I hope it hasn't given you a bad impression of us.

Charles It would have given a worse one if you hadn't stood up for poor Smike.

Nicholas And yet, if Snawley is his father, then he is in the right.

Charles The wisdom of Solomon, Nicholas. Should the boy go to the blood parent, or the guardian who loves him and makes him happy? Surely, we know the answer, don't we?

Nicholas You're very kind. Thank you for trusting us ... me.

Charles I trust you well enough that, with your permission, I wish to employ you on a confidential and delicate mission.

Nicholas Certainly. Anything.

Charles The object of this mission is a young lady.

Nicholas A young lady?

Charles A very beautiful young lady. (*Pause*) You accidentally saw a young lady take an envelope from me in the employment bureau. Perhaps you have forgotten?

Nicholas I remember — although you asked me not to at the time.

Charles She is the daughter of a lady, whom I once loved very deeply. But that lady married her choice, and I wish to God I could say her life was as happy as I hoped it would have been with me. Her husband began as a lively man-about-town, but his habits lead them into financial calamity. She sickened and came to see me a few months before she died. Her daughter was still quite young, and she appealed to me to guard the child who might have been mine. I gave her some money, which has been put aside as an inheritance for the blessed day when that young lady's father passes on. That girl is the beautiful young lady you saw. Her father is desperately ill with a diseased heart, and she, more caring than he deserves, came to me to ask for money to relieve his discomfort. That was our business at the bureau.

Nicholas What a sad story.

Charles I have received a note from her to say the small amount I gave last month is now exhausted. She needs more. Medicine is expensive, true — but I doubt his requirements are confined to medicaments. Her father is a volatile creature. If he knew their charity came from me, he would punish her for it. Hence, we have devised a scheme whereby he believes the gifts are earned from work as a seamstress and as a maker of small silk and paper ornaments.

Nicholas What do you want me to do?

Charles I want you to visit their home, and to present payment for certain items you will say were commissioned for your mistress.

Nicholas Of course.

Charles Their name is Bray. Here is the envelope. The address is written on it.

Nicholas And, well ... could you tell me her first name?

Charles Madeline.

SCENE 9

Noggs's Office

There is a cupboard on stage. Noggs is marching up and down in his small office, obviously agitated

Noggs It's five minutes to three. And I had my breakfast at eight. "Don't go 'til I come back." Day after day. "Don't go 'til I come back." Here he is, and somebody with him. Now it'll be, don't go until I'm finished with this gentleman. Well, if I can't get past him, then I'm getting in here (*he indicates the cupboard*) and leaving him to look after himself.

Noggs gets into the cupboard

Ralph enters followed by Gride — a wizened, avaricious old man

Ralph Noggs! Now, where's he gone? Noggs! He's gone for his dinner, though I told him not to.

Gride Oh, it's very nice.

Ralph No it isn't. So, what do you want?

Gride No time to chat over bygone days?

Ralph Supposing I particularly want to remember our bygones. Come on?

Gride Time costs money. That's our trade, of course. (*Pause*) What would you say to me, if I were to tell you that I am going to be married?

Ralph To some old hag?

Gride No, no. To a young, beautiful girl — fresh, lovely. And not yet nineteen.

Ralph What's the girl's name?

Gride You always were quick. Suspect a plot, eh?

Ralph Can't see what else would bring such a thing about.

Gride Still sharp, Nickleby. Her name — there's nobody to overhear us, is there? I should have been very uncomfortable if Mr Noggs ...

Ralph So should I. Curse Mr Noggs — get on with it.

Gride Curse him, indeed. Her name is Madeline Bray. You remember Madeline Bray? Daughter of Walter Bray, who used his handsome wife so badly.

Ralph Oh, him. It's his daughter, is it? So you're to marry the daughter of a ruined "dashing man". You obviously want some help from me — or you wouldn't be here.

Gride Indeed, some help with a little plan I have in mind to help bring this union about. I want a backer in this matter — someone who can talk and urge, and press a point — which is what you're good at. I am a poor, timid creature.

Ralph And what's in it for me?

Gride Bray is in debt to me for one thousand and seven hundred pounds.

Ralph And to me for nine hundred and seventy-five.

Gride But his bankruptcy means we'd neither of us expect to be paid this side of hell. So, I have offered myself to Bray as son-in-law in return for not only releasing him from debt, but also awarding him an allowance and property sufficient to keep him in comfort for the rest of his days.

Ralph All right, you get the girl. But where's the profit? You're not telling me it's love.

Gride You'll remember there was a certain matter of a will, which old Bray touted as a guarantee against his borrowing. A will made out by the girl's mother, in which she intended to secure the child's future. He'd kept it a secret from the girl, who stands to receive a tidy sum, but only if either old Bray dies, or she gets married. Now, I have that will safely locked away — on his behalf, so to speak. And of course, under the law, a wife's property goes to her husband. And if that's me ... well, then ...

Ralph I see. (*Pause*) If you married this girl without my involvement, then you'd have to pay off my debt anyway — otherwise you couldn't set her father free. So, as things stand I won't be gaining by my involvement. I want five hundred pounds clear profit on top of the debt. And I want you to sign a bond that you'll pay off both sums before noon on the day of your marriage. Those are my terms.

Gride Agreed. I knew it would turn out like this.

Ralph Good, then. Let's go to the chop house. You can buy us an early supper in celebration of the coming nuptials.

Gride I won't eat, thank you.

Ralph Then you can watch me.

The two men leave

A rather stiff Newman Noggs creeps out of his hiding place

Noggs Well, and I've lost my appetite. They can have their dinner, and what they've got planned makes them cannibals, for sure. Poor girl. If only I knew her. Ah, well, I can't do anything about it. Nor can I help any of the hundred against whom such vile tricks are plotted every day.

SCENE 10

The Bray residence

Walter Bray sits in a chair. A small table next to him carries a selection of medicine bottles. Madeline sits at another table concentrating on a small watercolour painting

Nicholas half opens the door, realizes they don't know he's there, so knocks discreetly

Bray Who's this? Madeline? What does he want? Who let you up here?

Nicholas I'm sorry to interrupt. The door was open.

Madeline I believe ——

Bray (*mimicking her*) You always "believe". You sound like your mother — infernally polite. Infernally even-tempered and "civilized". Now, what is it you want?

Nicholas I am here on behalf of my employer, who was well-pleased with the two drawings. I have the payment, in full. She also wishes to confirm the order for the silk flowers. So, the deposit is here too. (*He puts an envelope on the table*)

Bray Check to make sure the money is right.

Madeline It's quite right, Papa. I'm sure.

Bray Dammit. Give it to me, if you're too well-bred to count it. How can you be sure if you don't look at a thing. Five pounds. Is that right?

Madeline Quite right.

Bray Where's the girl? Tell her to get me a newspaper. To buy some grapes. And another bottle of that wine I had last week. I forget half of what I want. But no matter, she can always go out again. Tell her to get those first. Those things first. Why are you still here? Do you want a receipt?

Nicholas It's of no matter, sir.

Bray That's the first sensible thing you said. It's of no matter, all right.

Nicholas I merely meant that we shall be having many dealings, and the matter of a receipt can wait.

Bray "Dealings"? We'll have as many dealings as we like. And none if we don't like. I don't want pity from a petty tradesman. I'm a gentleman, and this is a gentleman's daughter. And mind you remember it.

Nicholas When shall I call again?

Madeline Not for a while. Three or four weeks. I can do without.

Bray Why? How are we to do without? Three or four weeks!

Nicholas I will come soon. To check on your progress.

Madeline That will be kind.

Bray What did he say?

Madeline (*whispering*) Would you step aside, please?

They move away from Bray

Did Charles Cheeryble send you?

Nicholas Yes.

Madeline And what's your name?

Nicholas Nicholas Nickleby.

Madeline I know that look, Mr Nickleby. I can see you pity me, but you mustn't. This man is my father, and I owe him my love. The fact he's weak and selfish means he deserves to be loved all the more, because he is so flawed and hates himself so much. We live a frugal existence, but have a roof and rarely miss a meal. So I can't — I won't say I am in want. My father did his best, but it wasn't good enough. He can't be judged for that, because it was his best. Do you see? I have been given a little education, and a few of my mother's talents, and he punishes me because he loved her but couldn't show it. That's our life, Mr Nickleby. Don't judge it cruelly. He will die soon, and I will miss him more then I can say.

Bray What? Whispering?

Nicholas Goodbye, sir.

Nicholas and Madeline both raise their palms to each other in a discreet wave

Bray Goodbye and good riddance. Where is that girl!

SCENE 11

Bray remains at his table, alone. The following scene takes place in and around him, as if two scenes can co-exist in the same space without reference to one another

The characters of Nicholas and Brooker are played by the same actor. So, in this scene, when Smike spots Brooker, there will be some sleight of hand which allows Smike to look into Nicholas's face and see someone else

Nicholas is walking away from Madeline Bray's house. He is deep in thought, and surprised when Smike ambushes him

Nicholas Smike! What are you doing here?
Smike I waited for you? Thought you could do with the company. (*Pause, while he coughs*) And I missed you.
Nicholas Stop. Look up, Smike. You really are very pale, today. That cough doesn't seem to be getting better. We'll have you to the doctor tomorrow.
Smike No. No doctor. The doctor always made the boys worse.
Nicholas It's a pleasant evening. Let's walk along. Guess what, Smike?
Smike What?
Nicholas I think I might have fallen in love today.
Smike What does it feel like?
Nicholas Oh, heavens! What questions you do ask. All right. Um. It's a fluttery feeling, in here. Like one is expecting a special letter, or it's Christmas Eve. And there's a worry up here. As if today's sighting might be snatched away, and one might never see her again.
Smike Ah. I see.
Nicholas And there is absolutely not a shadow of a doubt that the person one has met is the most beautiful one has ever seen. Smike. Maybe one day it'll happen to you.
Smike Do you fall in love often?
Nicholas Not like this. I don't think. Heavens, look at the sun over the city. Huge and red.

Smike coughs again. More seriously this time

Nicholas Are you all right?
Smike Yes. A smut in my throat, I think.

Smike sees Brooker standing watching them from across the street

Nicholas Smike? What can you see?
Smike (*trembling*) That's him. I didn't think I knew him. But I do. That's him.

A coach passes and momentarily obscures Brooker. When it has passed, Brooker has gone

Smike That must mean I'm going to die.
Nicholas What are you talking about?
Smike Remember I told you about the boy who died? He saw his friends from the past. And his mother kissed him.
Nicholas Who was it? Who do you think you saw?
Smike Him. The man who left me at Yorkshire. All those years ago.
Nicholas Was it Sawney?
Smike No. Definitely not.

Pause — Smike looks into Nicholas's eyes

Do you really think I might fall in love?

SCENE 12

Nicholas walks off the space as Ralph enters — the two eye each other as they move. Gride and Smike do the same. Bray also enters

Ralph (*immersed in conversation with Bray*) You haven't heard me out. You could still shine in society, with many distinguished years ahead of you. That is, if you lived in freer air, and under brighter skies, and chose your own companions. Gaiety is your element. You shone in it before. Fashion and freedom for you. France, and an annuity that would support you in luxury. Transferred to a new existence. And what's the alternative? To live on as you do now. And what to look forward to but the graveyard — and when — two years maybe. And what of your daughter? This match would serve her financially. And her new husband? Between us, how long will he last? And whatever short-term disappointment she might feel, well ... that will seem nothing for her to have been made very rich, desirable — and still be in her prime. Besides, if you stay as you are — once that heart carries you off — who will be left to make her happy? Surely the relatives of your dead wife — with all their tut-tuts about you ringing on through the years. And what pleasure it will give them to rescue her from your memory.
Bray Shhh! I hear her at the door.

Madeline enters. She is instantly concerned to see the two strangers — assuming it means her father must be ill

Madeline What's the matter? Has he been unwell? Who are you?

Ralph A sudden spasm. He is quite well now.

Bray Madeline, it was nothing.

Madeline But you had a spasm yesterday. It's terrible to see you in such pain. Can't I do anything?

Bray You are very tired, my dear.

Madeline Don't worry about me.

Bray Indeed you are. You do too much. This wretched life, my love, of daily labour and fatigue, is more than you can bear, I am sure it is. Poor Madeline.

Ralph You will communicate with us again, won't you?

Bray Yes. Yes. In a week. Give me a week.

Ralph Very well, one week from today. Good-evening, Miss Madeline.

Bray Will you shake hands, Mr Gride? I don't doubt you mean well. If I owe you money, then it isn't your fault. My dear. Will you shake hands with Mr Gride?

Madeline shrinks from Gride's distasteful goblin-like appearance. But she obediently offers her hand. He takes it and bends to kiss it. His thick saliva makes gluey strings as he pulls back. It is as though she is defiled by his touch

Ralph and Gride step forward. They play the following with the tableau of Bray and Madeline behind them

Gride What does the giant say to the pigmy. Isn't she a dainty morsel?

Ralph Yes ... I mean, she may be.

Gride What's the matter with you? We did well.

Ralph By which you mean we did ill. Don't ask me about what we did. I have ... no use for beauty.

Gride But she appreciated me, don't you think?

Ralph I wouldn't say she was overly loving. I'm sure it's done, Gride. Did you see the effort Bray was making to persuade himself? Yes, he's stuffed, decorated and in the oven. She saw something in him too. He was changed, wasn't he? Parents, eh? What rule says because you have a child, that means you have to put yourself second? If there is one, it's not in Bray's book. Nor mine, either.

SCENE 13

The Nickleby residence

*Mrs Nickleby is snoozing with a book in her lap. Miss La Creevy bustles
in, waking Mrs Nickleby, who immediately pretends she is reading*

Mrs Nickleby I was just resting my eyes while contemplating his point.
But, it's no use, "four legs good, two legs bad". I can't get the hang of
it. I like a book where it's clear how the story will turn out. No idea
with this one.

Miss La Creevy I saw young Mr Cheeryble on the road. He was resting
a while, looking at his watch. I'd say he'll be knocking at that door
any time, now. But where's my nice young friend?

Mrs Nickleby Ah. Where is Smike? He was here this instant. Well,
now. He is the strangest creature. Last Tuesday — was it Tuesday?
Yes it was. The very last time young Mr Frank Cheeryble was here.
Last Tuesday Smike went off in exactly the same strange way, at the
very moment the knock came at the door. And the oddest thing is that
he does not go to bed. Therefore it cannot be that he is tired. I went
upstairs last Tuesday hours after him, and I found that he had been
sitting moping in the dark all that time.

Frank Cheeryble knocks at the door

*Miss La Creevy admits him. Kate suddenly appears as if she has been
waiting for the visitor*

Frank Good-evening, Mrs Nickleby. Miss La Creevy.

Mrs Nickleby I am so sorry, Nicholas is not at home.

Frank Oh, it's of no matter. Just a pleasure to see you all — really. Ah,
Kate.

Mrs Nickleby Kate, my dear, you must be both Nicholas and yourself,
and entertain our visitor accordingly.

Kate Mother, what strange things you do say.

Frank Miss Nickleby need be but herself, and that will provide fully
for the effort of the journey. And certainly, I wouldn't have her play
anyone else, for all the world.

SCENE 14

The Races

The Fop is played by the same actor who plays Nicholas

Verisopht and Hawk are at the races, doffing their hats to passers-by. Hawk is obviously uncomfortable

Fop Ah! Hawk! How d'ye do, old fellow. And how are you getting on, now?

Hawk Quite well.

Fop That's right. Stout fellow. How d'ye do, Verisopht. He's a little pulled down, so to speak. Off his perch, so to speak. Our friend here. Rather out of condition, eh?

Verisopht He's in very good condition. Nothing the matter with him.

Fop Upon my soul, I'm glad to hear it. It's really uncommonly bold of you.

Hawk What is?

Fop Why, showing yourself in public so soon, of course.

Hawk What do you mean?

Fop Well, of course, you know the rights and wrongs of the affair. The rest of us only have the papers to go by. So, obvious question — why didn't you put them straight? Give your side of the whole business. Tell the truth about the lady in the case, and what type she is, and so on.

Hawk (*staring back at the young man with his eyes narrowed*) Look in the papers again. Tomorrow. No, next day. Will you do that for me?

Fop What should I look for, eh?

Hawk That's as much as I'm saying. Good-day. (*Turning his back on the Fop*)

Verisopht What did you mean? About the p-p-papers?

Hawk Don't worry, I won't give him a murder case to read about. But it shall be damned near it, and I tell you, I'll be surprised if he can walk unaided for the rest of his days.

Verisopht Are you making this up? Is it just bravado? Or do you intend to do harm to the girl's brother?

Hawk He marked me, boy. And broke my bones.

Verisopht I forbid you to d-d-do ... whatever it is you are planning.

Hawk I d-d-don't believe my ears.

Verisopht You heard what I said. (*Pause*) Look, we're companions, and all. I don't want to fall out. But on this I will have to be r-r-resolute, I really will.

Hawk And will you try to prevent me?

Verisopht Y-yes, if I can.

Hawk You owe me money. And in a very little while, you'll owe me more. You're weak, and stupid. Why else do you think I tolerate your company? Now, if you want us to get on — just mind your own business, and leave me to mine.

Verisopht This is mine. I am compromised by my association with your plots against that young lady. And it remains a question for me how far you took things when I and others we're not about to keep you in check. (*He grabs Hawk by the arm*) Stand still. I won't have you walk away from me. I warn you. Do not make an attempt against this fellow whose sister you degraded. I said, don't walk away. If you do, I shall raise a cry against you.

Hawk You are a foolish nothing whose only place in the world has come by accident, and yet you're so useless you can barely hang on to the good cards fate dealt you. Without me, you would already be bankrupt. Now shut up, and let go of me.

Verisopht strikes Hawk across the face with his gloves. Nothing happens, so he does it again. He raises his hand for a third blow

Don't you dare, or I'll kill you right here. Contact your representative, young man. Sunrise. The meadows opposite Twickenham.

SCENE 15

Gride's office

Gride is at his desk, poring over a ledger

Noggs taps gently at the open door and enters. He has a letter

Gride Ah! Mr Noggs! What news do you bring for me?
Noggs A letter. From Mr Nickleby.

Gride reads

Gride Yes. I'll write a line. I'm — I'm rather flurried. The news is ——
Noggs Bad?
Gride No, Mr Noggs. Good. The very best of news. Sit down while I write an answer.

Noggs sits at the desk

  Gride bustles off in search of pen and paper

Ralph enters upstage and recites the contents of the letter

Ralph "Gride. I saw Bray again this morning and he proposed tomorrow for the wedding. There's no point in dragging things out. Bray has no objection, and the plan is to take the girl by surprise. He continues breaking her down. Her loyalty to him is precisely the weapon he uses against her. Be ready for seven in the morning, tomorrow. I'll pick you up, and we'll catch them sleepy-eyed. Yours, Ralph Nickleby."

Gride enters with the reply

Noggs lifts his eyes from the note and fixes his gaze in the middle distance

Gride Do you see anything in particular, Mr Noggs?
Noggs Only a cobweb.
Gride Oh, is that all?
Noggs There's a fly in it.
Gride There's your reply, Mr Noggs. Now, before you go — shall we have a toast?
Noggs Look sharp. Bearer waits.

Gride pours a minute amount of red wine into two miniature glasses

Gride We'll drink to a lady.
Noggs To the ladies!

Gride arrests the journey of the glass to Noggs's lips

Gride No, no, Mr Noggs. A lady. One lady in particular. Little Madeline. That's the toast. To little Madeline.
Noggs Madeline! God help her!

SCENE 16

Next to the Thames

Pyke and Verisopht stand in the morning mist on open ground next to the Thames

Pyke Shivering? Are you cold?
Verisopht Rather.
Pyke Did you sleep last night? Or claret and cards?

Verisopht Cards.
Pyke Best thing.

Pluck approaches carrying a box containing guns

Pluck We assume an apology is not forthcoming.
Pyke Absolutely not.
Pluck Right-o. I have the guns here. Choose please.

Verisopht takes a gun from the box

Pluck Well done. Two minutes.

He walks away

Verisopht Look at the trees.
Pyke What about 'em?
Verisopht The shimmering leaves. So loud. And the clouds rushing
behind them. It really is a beautiful spot, isn't it?
Pyke They're ready.

Verisopht walks off

Pyke remains on stage watching the action

Pluck (*off*) That's the range, gentlemen. When I drop the handkerchief,
you may fire in your own time.

There is a long pause, then a single loud report

Pluck enters

Pluck He's gone. I call you to witness this was fairly done. I must get
Hawk away from here. We'll push for Chichester and cross to France
tonight. This is a bad business, and it'll be worse for all of us, if we
delay. What about you?
Pyke Ages since I visited my mother. Do you think Nairobi is far
enough, until things cool off? (*Pause*) Strikes one, don't you think
— that the errand boy will probably never know the favour young
Verisopht did him.

SCENE 17

Ralph's office

Ralph is pacing his office, obviously keen to receive Gride's reply. Noggs enters with it

Ralph You've been a long time.
Noggs He took a long time.
Ralph Give me the reply. And don't disappear. I want a word with you.

Noggs gives it to him. Ralph reads it
    Good. That's settled. Now for you, Noggs. Tell me, who was that man you were talking to in the street last night?
Noggs I don't know.
Ralph Then you'd better refresh your memory.
Noggs I don't know him. Meaning, he's nothing to me. He came here twice and asked for you. You were out. He gave the name of Brooker.
Ralph I know. What then?
Noggs He wants to see you face to face. Says you'll be certain to hear him out.
Ralph And what did you say to that?
Noggs I said he might catch you in the street, if he only wants to talk to you. Then he said, he wants to be in a locked room with you, where he can speak without fear, and he'll soon make you change your tone.
Ralph If he contacts you again, hand him over to the police. Tell 'em he tried to extort money with threats. I'll take care of the legal side. We'll have him back in prison for good. Do you understand me?
Noggs I hear.
Ralph Do it then. And I'll pay you what it's worth. Now, be off.

SCENE 18

Nicholas is returning home from work

Noggs ambushes him in the street

Nicholas Newman! What fun. Where have you been?
Noggs About my duties. For your uncle. Depressing.
Nicholas I shouldn't wonder. Bide your time, Newman. Now, what shall we do to blow away the day? You know, I was thinking about you that very moment.

Noggs And I of you. I needed to tell you, I think our time might soon be at hand. I think I'm about to discover something important.

Nicholas Excellent! What's the business?

Noggs It's some secret which shrouds your uncle. I have found a man called Brooker — or rather, he found me — and he knows more than he cares to tell right now.

Nicholas Marvellous.

Noggs Well, let's leave it there. I can't say any more just now, because I don't know any more. Come on, talk to me about this girl again. Take my mind off today.

Nicholas She's beautiful. And fiercely loyal to a father who doesn't deserve it.

Noggs Painfully familiar. (*He freezes*) It couldn't be ——

Nicholas What's the matter?

Noggs Tell me her name.

Nicholas Madeline.

Noggs Oh, dear God! Madeline? And her other name? Say her other name.

Nicholas Bray.

Noggs We cannot stand by while this unnatural marriage takes place without raising an attempt to save her.

Nicholas What are you talking about? Marriage? You're mad.

Nogs Then you don't know that tomorrow, by means of your Uncle Ralph, she will be married to a man as bad as him? She will be sacrificed, flesh and soul — yes, in flesh and in soul — to a wizened old usurer who has entrapped her father, and forces the wedding.

Nicholas Oh, God. What shall I do? Newman. You must find that man. Find Brooker and make him tell you everything. Do it now.

After a moment's hesitation, Nicholas runs from the stage

Noggs (*to the audience*) Stop him! He'll do something desperate. He'll murder somebody. Stop him, and save him! Stop thief! Thief! THIEF!

SCENE 19

The Bray residence

Ralph and Gride discover Bray sitting in a chair, his face ashen in the dawn light. Gride hangs back at a discreet distance

Bray Hush! She was very ill last night. I thought she would break her heart. She is dressed.

Ralph She is ready, is she?

Bray Quite ready.

Ralph And not planning to delay us with any young lady devices — fainting and so forth.

Bray She may be trusted. We have spoken, and she is at peace with her sacrifice.

Ralph (*cynically*) Oh, God save us!

Bray Indeed. This is a cruel thing to do.

Ralph (*in confidence to Bray*) Look at him. (*Meaning Gride*) If he were younger, it might be cruel. But he'll die soon and leave her a rich widow. She can choose the next husband herself.

Bray I must go upstairs. To finish dressing. And when I come down, I'll bring Madeline with me.

Bray picks up a piece of paper and crumples it in his fist, then leaves. Ralph turns to Gride

Ralph Mark my words, Gride. He'll be dead by the next quarter. Wake yourself up a bit. At least try to look a decade or two younger.

Gride It's damned early, Nickleby. Bones don't work 'til noon, at least.

Nicholas and Kate enter the room

Ralph Across my path at every turn. Wherever I go. Do what I may. He comes!

Gride stares at the threesome

Gride God, you're three of a kind. Out of the same mould.

Nicholas I have come here to save your victim, if I can. You are, in every action of your life, a scoundrel and a liar. Here I stand, and will wait until I have thwarted you.

Ralph You, girl. Get out of here, or you'll suffer the same marks I'll put across his insolent face.

Kate I won't go away. If you do injure me, it will be in keeping with your customary cowardice, and nothing compared to the black despair you made me feel the day I came to you for help, and was rejected.

Ralph Go on, you silly girl!

Nicholas You threaten, but I've got thirty years on you. Attack me, and I swear I'll put you down.

Ralph Gride. Call Bray down here.

Madeline enters. She is calm, and deathly pale. Her stillness settles the atmosphere of the room. She has a note crumpled in her hand

Madeline He is dead.

Nicholas Who?
Madeline My father. He need not have climbed the stairs. I was bringing his coat. Why did he climb the stairs?

Kate goes to Madeline

Kate You must come home to us. There. Cry if you must. You can cry.
Ralph I ——
Gride Quiet, Nickleby. Don't say anything.
Kate What's that? Let me see.

She takes the note from Madeline's hand, and passes it to Nicholas, who reads out loud

Nicholas "Gride. Nickleby. Both your debts are paid in the great debt of nature. I have made report of your planned fraud concerning my late wife's will. My written account is sent to the authorities."
Ralph This man claims his wife, and he shall have her.
Nicholas For heaven's sake, man. Stop struggling. The tide has turned. Your day is past, and night is coming on.
Ralph My curse. My bitter and deadly curse upon you, boy.
Nicholas Your world is fabricated by spies, who know no allegiance — least of all to you. The structures you have raised are crumbling. (*He moves away from the door*) Now go, both of you. And set your affairs in order as best you may.

Gride scurries out

Ralph walks away, as if in a daze

SCENE 20

The Cheerybles' business premises

Nicholas is engaged in animated conversation with Charles. Smike sits in the centre of the room, unnoticed, as if in a different space

Nicholas It's such a shame.
Charles Tell us what the doctor has said about Smike.
Nicholas He's so worn out and emaciated, it's painful to look at him. The disease is so far advanced. I didn't know what carried so many of Squeers's boys off, but now it's clear.
Ned Please, Nicholas. What did the doctor say?

Nicholas That his last hope is to be immediately removed from London. I told him about Devon, and the doctor said our part of the West Country was exactly what he needs.

Charles And so, is a cure really possible?

Nicholas The doctor said it was unlikely, and whoever accompanies him must be ready for the worst.

Charles Well, there's no question, then. This boy shall not die if there are means available to us to prevent it.

Ned Nicholas, I am granting you an indefinite leave, and I want you to draw an hundred pounds from the front office. Smike and yourself are to depart for Devon immediately. You will use the funds to rent a property as close to your former family home as is possible.

Charles I know, from what you have said, this will please Smike. The boy so longs to have a past like the rest of us. Goodbye, Nicholas.

Ned I shan't expect to see you until the matter is resolved ... for the better, I hope.

Charles retires from the stage and Nicholas joins the now animated, weakened Smike

Nicholas See, they are at the corner of the lane, still waving. And there's Kate — poor Kate, who you said you couldn't bear to say goodbye to — waving her handkerchief.

Smike Is Mr Frank beside her?

Nicholas Oh, yes. He's there. Smike, please wave to them.

Smike I can't. Can you still see her? Is she still there?

Nicholas Oh, yes. She's waving. I'll wave for both of us, shall I? Please don't cry, Smike. You will see them all again.

Smike In heaven. I humbly pray. In heaven.

SCENE 21

Ralph's office

Ralph sits at his desk reading a letter, recently arrived

Ralph It says the worst has happened. Hawk has fled the country. Two days ago he raised funds on his house in order to finance the escape. That house was already mortgaged to me for ten thousand pounds, upon which he was paying me double interest. Now the house is seized by the Crown, against the debts of the fugitive. Ten thousand pounds! How many years of pinching and sleepless nights? I could have enjoyed myself like them. But I kept my money close. Kept to silence, alone, in the night. To save, and scrimp, and save, and build my pile. I cringed to liberal, thoughtless, generous, dashing fools without the talent to save a sixpence against disaster. And now I'm ruined. Damn them. BURN THEM!

SCENE 22

Nicholas and Smike are on stage

Smike (*waking from a nightmare*) AAH!
Nicholas What is it, Smike? Calm down. It's only a dream.

Smike looks about him in a panic

Listen to me. It's just a dream.
Smike I saw him as plainly as I see you now. Hiding behind the tree. Swear you won't leave me alone. Not even for an instant.
Nicholas Who was it?
Smike Don't you remember me telling you about the man who first took me to school?
Nicholas Surely ...
Smike I raised my eyes just now towards that tree — and there he was, with his eyes fixed on me.
Nicholas Supposing he's even alive, then what would he be doing here? And how could you really know him after all this time?
Smike He was dusty from walking, and poorly dressed. It all came back to me. That wet night. His face when he left me. The parlour I was left in and the people that were there. I have thought of him in the day, and dreamt of him at night. I see his face, and I know it clearly. (*Pause*) You know, I am not afraid to die.
Nicholas Smike, please.
Smike I must tell you something first. I don't want there to be secrets between us. I hope you won't blame me.
Nicholas Why on earth should I blame you?
Smike You asked me why I sat so much alone. I couldn't help it, you see. I would have died to make her happy. It broke my heart when ... Although I know he loves her dearly.
Nicholas Kate? Is that who you mean?
Smike Yes. Please don't be angry.
Nicholas Oh, Smike. Of course I'm not angry. And who knows ... In a different life ...

Smike   Good. (*Pause*) Yesterday you showed me a corner of the churchyard where you said your father had found Kate sleeping, and had asked to have his body laid right there when he died. I have no family, but I would like it very much if I could be laid near that spot also, and then when your children come there to play about your father's grave, they will also be close to mine.

Nicholas   If it should ever happen, Smike. Yes, that's where you'll rest.

Smike   Beautiful gardens, stretched out ...

Nicholas   Yes, it's a very nice spot.

Smike   Filled with figures of men, women and many children ...

Nicholas   What?

Smike   With light on their faces.

He has died

SCENE 23

Ralph's office at Golden Square

Ralph is alone and unwell

Ralph   What is it that hangs over me? I can't shake it off. I have never pampered myself. Never moped and pined, and yielded to fancies. But what can a man do without sleep? Night after night, without rest. If I sleep, I dream of detested faces. When I'm awake, I am haunted by the shadow of ... I don't know what. I must have rest. One night's unbroken rest, and I would be a man again. (*Looking about him*) This is strange. Noon and Noggs not here. I ought to throw some temptation his way, something he couldn't resist. Then I could have him arrested and transported with irons on his leg — and I would be rid of his prying.

Ned Cherryble knocks at the door

What hour do you call this, Noggs? It's not locked. Let yourself in, and be quick!

Ned enters

Ralph   This is an unexpected favour, sir.

Ned   And an unwelcome one, no doubt.

Ralph   Plainly, sir.

Ned   Mr Nickleby, it is an errand of mercy that brings me here. Pray, let me discharge it.

Ralph I show no mercy, and I ask for none. (*Pause*) Go on then, sir. I'll be patient. Remember there are laws. Take care what you say, or I shall prove it.

Ned Last night I was witness to a confession given by the man Snawley.

Ralph And what may his confession have to do with me?

Ned This is your strategy, I suppose. To deny what is apparent. (*Pause*) Well, all right. Squeers has been arrested. Finally a loving parent — although "loving" too late, perhaps — yes, finally a parent has stepped forward to make a case against Squeers for neglect. In order to fend off the full weight of the law, Squeers has made a confession of his involvement with many schemes, including yours to engineer Smike's abduction under the pretence that Snawley is his father. Snawley was himself arrested on the instant, and has confirmed your part in the affair. Furthermore, Gride, hearing of events, has come forward to offer testimony of your efforts to help deprive Madeline Bray of her inheritance.

Ralph I see. Do you imagine I have no experience of the law and lawyers?

Ned I said I came here with mercy in mind. We would not have an old rogue like you disgrace your near relations. I entreat you to retire from London and take shelter some place where you will be safe from the consequences of your wicked designs.

Ralph Do you think you shall so easily crush me? I thank you for disclosing your schemes, which I am now prepared for. Try me, and I shall spit on your fair words and false dealings, and dare you, provoke you, taunt you, to do to me the very worst you can. Now get out!

SCENE 24

The Nickleby residence

Nicholas has returned to his family. He has just told them of Smike's death. Mrs Nickleby and Kate are upset at the news

Mrs Nickleby I am sure I have lost the best, the most zealous, and most attentive creature that has ever been a companion to me in life — putting you, my dear Nicholas, and Kate, and your poor papa, and that well-behaved nurse who ran away with the linen and the twelve small forks, to one side, of course. Of all the even-tempered, attached and faithful beings that ever lived, I believe he was the most even-tempered, attached and faithful. To look around the garden now, that he took so much pride in, or to go into his room and see it filled with his little trinkets — I can't bear it. I can't, really. I'll be in my room. Please leave me alone with my thoughts. But not for too long.

She goes

Kate She means what she says. We all feel it. Seeing you come back alone. But what better is there, than to know his last days were peaceful and happy? (*Pause*) What's the matter? That is true, isn't it?

Nicholas Yes. Of course.

Kate I can't tell you how glad I am to see you home again.

Nicholas Kate. I want you to know that I am in love with Madeline Bray.

Kate Of course. That's obvious.

Nicholas And do you approve?

Kate Of course I do.

Nicholas Then I shall set about the task of trying to prove to her that she should love me in return.

Kate If the indications are anything to go by, then I expect you will find she's not too difficult to convince.

Nicholas And what about Frank? His intentions were clear enough.

Kate And remain so. And I shall accept him.

Nicholas I'm very happy for you. (*Pause*) So, our world is about to change, isn't it? For the better, do you think?

Kate Yes. I do. Although, despite the trials which have beset us, I feel we found something very valuable, which is not granted to everyone.

Nicholas I do love you, Kate.

Kate And I love you, Nicholas.

SCENE 25

Ralph's office

Ralph sits alone at his desk. The room is dark. Charles Cheeryble enters

Charles Mr Nickleby? (*Pause*) That is you, is it? Shall I switch on the light?

Ralph No.

Charles Mr Nickleby, are you all right?

Ralph What's that to you? Why are you here again? I told you to stay away.

Charles I know you did. But Newman Noggs has come to me, accompanied by someone you know. And, although I hesitate to confront you with a terrible truth, I'm afraid I must.

Ralph Still harking on the business of the half-wit? Surely you've got something better to come at me with by now.

Charles Not harking on. Smike, poor fellow, is dead. He died of consumption just two days ago.
Ralph Then he's out of the picture and shouldn't vex either of us, should he?

Newman Noggs enters

Ralph Ah, there you are. So, you've changed masters, have you? A fickle familiar, eh? You're even more of a fool than I took you for, Mr Cheeryble. To recruit a fellow like this who would sell his soul — if he had one — for a drink, and whose every word is a lie.
Noggs "A fellow like this". Who made me a fellow like this? I am a ruined man, who has not always been what I am.
Charles Gently, Newman. You said you wouldn't. There's someone else here to see you.
Ralph And who's that outside the door? My nephew, is it? He brought you intelligence, did he? And no doubt wants to see me prostrated and overwhelmed by it. But I tell you Nicholas, I'll be a sharp thorn to wound you, and to poison that wound, for a long time to come.

Brooker steps forward in to the room

Brooker You take me for your nephew, eh? Well, you'll wish I were him.
Ralph What's he doing here? He's a convict. A common thief.
Charles Please, I think you must hear what he has to tell you.
Brooker That boy you were just speaking about.
Ralph Who is now in his grave, and whose presence in this discourse is nothing but a bore? Yes? What about him?
Brooker So help me, God in Heaven — that boy was your only son. (*Pause*) I offer no excuses for myself. I am long past that. Perhaps, because I was harshly used, and so driven half out of my nature — that's perhaps why I behaved against nature. But no more of that. I'm not looking for sympathy. What do you remember?

There is no reply from Ralph

It's twenty years, now, since you wound a debt around a hard-drinking gentleman who squandered his fortune. He had a sister — who wasn't a girl anymore, but was pretty — and due to inherit some considerable property in time. And you married her, didn't you? But you kept it a secret because the will forbade her to marry without the brother's consent. And he wouldn't give it, so you waited for him to break his neck. Meanwhile, the result of this quiet marriage was a son. The child was given to a nurse, and the mother saw him only very occasionally, because you would not allow it. But you never went near the mite —

in order to avoid raising suspicion. When you had been married nearly
seven years, your wife eloped with a younger man. The secret was
out, and whether you couldn't be bothered with the child — or more
likely wanted to punish his mother by putting him where he'd never be
found — you entrusted the child to me, with the instruction he should
never be found. And now begins what you don't know. I brought the
child home to my own house. Neglect had made him very sickly, and I
called a doctor, who said he must be removed to clean air, or he would
die. That's what gave me the idea. When you contacted me six weeks
later, I told you the boy was dead and buried. Despite yourself, you
were upset at that, and gave me an allowance in his memory — which
I used to finance the boy until your service drove me into prison six
years ago. I took the child to the Yorkshire school run by Squeers. To
this day, I carry the guilt upon my soul. And it gets heavier. There is
no reparation I can make. I am older than my years in misery and care.
But what I feel can be nothing compared to you who have hunted and
persecuted your own child, have caused him unimaginable pain, and
hurried him to death.

There is a long pause

Charles Mr Nickleby?
Ralph (*so quiet, he can barely be heard*) Leave me alone.
Charles You should come with us.
Ralph Leave me. Please.

The two men file out, leaving Ralph to his thoughts

Smike enters

Smike Long, lonely nights in a small high room.

Ralph slowly raises his head to look at the ceiling

And in the ceiling, a small window, through which the moon sometimes
stared. And a big iron hook ... in the ceiling ... next to the latch of that
window.
Ralph (*after a pause*) Is that really all you can remember?
Smike (*offering a pitiful shrug of his shoulders*) Pain and fear. That's
all. Pain and fear is all there is for me.

*Ralph opens the drawer of his desk and takes out a length of rope. He
stands on the desk, ties the rope to the hook then around his own neck*

It's over, and you can sleep now. So much effort. So difficult. No more frowns. We're all right. I'll look after you. Father.

Black-out

CURTAIN

FURNITURE AND PROPERTY LIST

In scenes where no furniture and property are specified, dressing may be left to the director's discretion.

ACT I

SCENE 2

Off stage: Cane, two open letters (in inside pocket) (**Squeers**)

SCENE 4

On stage: Chair

Off stage: Letter in envelope (in inside pocket) (**Nicholas**)

SCENE 5

On stage: Chair
Portrait
Paints

SCENE 6

On stage: Fence
Stone

SCENE 7

Personal: **Mrs Nickleby**: coin

SCENE 8

On stage: Book (for **Smike**)

Personal: **Mrs Nickleby**: coin

ACT II

SCENE 1

On stage: Three chairs

SCENE 2

On stage: Chair

SCENE 3

On stage: Sofa
              Book (for **Kate**)

SCENE 4

Personal: **Ralph**: letter

SCENE 5

Off stage: Jug of beer, glasses (**Crummles**)

SCENE 9

On stage: Make-up (for **Nicholas** and **Crummles**)

ACT III

SCENE 1

On stage: Two tables
              Chairs
              Mugs of beer

Personal: **Nicholas**: card (in coat pocket)
              Hawk: cane

SCENE 2

Off stage: Sealed letter (**Noggs**)

SCENE 3

On stage: Rows of vacancy cards

Personal: **Madeline**: handkerchief
                Charles: sealed envelope

SCENE 4

Personal: **Squeers**: walking stick

SCENE 5

On stage: Desk
                Chair

Personal: **Squeers**: walking stick

SCENE 9

On stage: Cupboard

SCENE 10

On stage: Chair
                Small table. *On it*: selection of medicine bottles
                Table. *On it*: small watercolour painting

SCENE 11

On stage: As before

SCENE 12

On stage: As before

SCENE 13

On stage: Chair
                Book (for **Mrs Nickleby**)

SCENE 14

Personal: **Verisopht**: gloves

SCENE 15

On stage: Desk. *On it*: ledger
                Red wine
                Glasses

Off stage: Letter (**Gride**)
                 Pen, paper (**Gride**)

Scene 16

Off stage: Box containing guns (**Pluck**)

Scene 19

On stage: Chair
                 Piece of paper

Off stage: Crumpled piece of paper (**Madeline**)

Scene 21

On stage: Chair
                 Desk
                 Letter

Scene 25

On stage: Chair
                 Desk with drawer containing length of rope

FIREARMS AND OTHER WEAPONS USED IN THEATRE PRODUCTIONS

With regards to the rules and regulations of firearms and other weapons used in theatre productions, we recommend that you read the Entertainment Information Sheet No. 20 (Health and Safety Executive).

This information sheet is one of a series produced in consultation with the Joint Advisory Committee for Broadcasting and the Performing Arts. It gives guidance on the management of weapons that are part of a production, including firearms, replicas and deactivated weapons.

This sheet may be downloaded from: www.hse.gov.uk. Alternatively, you can contact HSE Books, P O Box 1999, Sudbury, Suffolk, CO10 2WA Tel: 01787 881165 Fax: 01787 313995.

LIGHTING PLOT

Unless otherwise specified, atmospheric lighting appropriate to the scene

ACT I

Cue 1	**Nicholas**: "That's right." *Fade upstage lights*	(Page 7)
Cue 2	**Nicholas**: "... as I have done here." *Lights snap to a cold dawn*	(Page 15)

ACT II

Cue 3	**Noggs**: "Come in and sit down, Mr Smike." *Firelight*	(Page 19)
Cue 4	**Pluck**: "A talent, indeed." *Assembly is backlit, then bring up Lights*	(Page 23)
Cue 5	**Nicholas**: "And remember we're ... on a budget." *Firelight*	(Page 30)
Cue 6	To open ACT II, SCENE 6 *Footlights*	

ACT III

Cue 7	**Smike**: "I'll look after you. Father." *Black-out*	(Page 78)

EFFECTS PLOT

ACT I

No cues

ACT II

www.ingramcontent.com/pod-product-compliance
Lightning Source LLC
LaVergne TN
LVHW051751080426
835511LV00018B/3303